The Financial Progression System

Author/Editor: Rev. Darryl Bass

Electronic ISBN: 978-1-972115-17-6 (EPUB),
978-1-972115-34-3 (Kindle)
Paperback ISBN: 978-1-972115-18-3
Hardcover ISBN: 978-1-972115-19-0
Printed in the United States

The Library of Congress Control Number: 2026905830

Bass Publishing, LLC
Maywood, IL 60153

Disclaimer

The information contained in this book is for educational and informational purposes only. It is not intended as financial, legal, tax, medical, psychological, or professional advice. The author and publisher make no guarantees regarding the results that may be obtained from the use of this material.

All examples provided are illustrative and are not intended to represent or guarantee that any individual will achieve similar results. Personal growth, financial improvement, and life progression outcomes depend on individual effort, discipline, decisions, and circumstances.

Readers are encouraged to seek qualified professional advice regarding financial planning, legal matters, mental health, or other specialized areas before making decisions based on the information provided in this book.

The author and publisher disclaim any liability for any loss, risk, or damages, direct or indirect, that may arise from the use or application of the information contained herein.

By reading this book, you acknowledge that you are responsible for your own decisions, actions, and results.

Details in any stories and anecdotes have been changed to protect the identities of the person(s) involved.

Scripture quotations are taken from the King James Version of the Bible.

ACKNOWLEDGEMENTS

First and always, **all glory, honor, and praise belong to God**.

This work exists because of His grace, wisdom, and patience. Every insight, every principle, every system within these pages was shaped through prayer, lived experience, failure, correction, and divine instruction. Without God's guidance, this book would be empty information. With Him, it becomes transformation. *"Except the LORD build the house, they labour in vain that build it"* (Psalm 127:1a)

I acknowledge my family—those who stood beside me through seasons of sacrifice, long nights of writing, and moments when the vision was bigger than the resources. Your support, prayers, and belief gave this work oxygen. Thank you for enduring the journey with me and for trusting the assignment even when the outcome was not yet visible.

I extend deep gratitude to every client, student, church member, and individual who trusted me with their financial story. Your struggles, breakthroughs, questions, and victories shaped this system more than any textbook ever could. You are the reason this book speaks to real life instead of theory.

I also acknowledge mentors, teachers, coaches, and leaders—both named and unnamed—who poured wisdom into my life. Some taught me what to do. Others taught me what *not* to do. All of them contributed to the clarity found in these pages.

Finally, I acknowledge **you**, the reader. The fact that you picked up this book means something inside you refuses to accept financial confusion as your destiny. That courage matters. This book was written with you in mind.

DEDICATION

This book is dedicated to **every individual who has ever felt financially lost but refused to stay that way**.

To the person living paycheck to paycheck, wondering how hard work still feels like survival.

To the family burdened by debt, yet determined to break the cycle.

To the believer who loves God deeply but was never taught or does not understand the Biblical principles of how money works.

To the parent who wants to leave peace instead of pressure to the next generation.

To the dreamer who knows there must be more than financial stress and uncertainty.

This work is for you.

It is also dedicated to future generations—those who will never meet me, but who will live freer lives because someone before them chose discipline, wisdom, and intentionality. May this system help shift bloodlines from poverty to prosperity, from struggle to stewardship, from reaction to readiness, from survival to sovereignty.

About the Author

Reverend Darryl Bass is an author, teacher, pastor, and transformational coach dedicated to helping individuals and families build stronger lives spiritually, personally, and financially. With a background that includes service in the financial sector and years of ministry leadership, he brings together practical wisdom, real-world experience, and faith-centered insight to guide people toward lasting change.

As Assistant Pastor of Impact Church in Maywood, Illinois, Rev. Bass has committed his life to serving others with compassion, clarity, and purpose. His work extends far beyond the pulpit. He is known for empowering people through life coaching, financial education, spiritual encouragement, and systems designed to help individuals break cycles, gain direction, and build lasting stability.

Rev. Bass is also a devoted husband and father who deeply values faith, family, discipline, and legacy. His life and work reflect a commitment to helping people not only overcome present challenges, but also create a future marked by wisdom, stewardship, and generational impact.

An entrepreneur at heart, he has founded and developed multiple mission-driven ventures centered on financial literacy, debt freedom, personal growth, and community advancement. Through his teaching, writing, and program development, he has consistently focused on helping others improve their credit, increase income, eliminate debt, strengthen savings, prepare for retirement, and build a foundation that can bless future generations.

What sets Rev. Darryl Bass apart is his ability to connect principle with practice. His message is not merely about inspiration, but implementation. Whether writing about mindset, money, faith, legacy, or personal development, his goal is always the same: to equip people with the tools, wisdom, and confidence they need to move forward intentionally.

Through every book, Rev. Bass continues his mission of helping people rise above limitation, walk in purpose, and build lives that reflect both abundance and responsibility.

FOREWORD

Most financial books tell you **what** to do.
Few teach you **how to think** while doing it.

The Financial Progression System is different.

This book does not begin with money—it begins with *position.* It understands that before dollars move correctly, **people must move correctly**. Before accounts change, **mindsets must shift**. And before wealth is built, **clarity must be established**. If you haven't read the book The Life Progression System, I would suggest you stop here and go and read it first.

Rev. Darryl Bass does not approach finance as a salesman, a theorist, or a motivator chasing hype. He approaches it as a **strategist, teacher, and builder**—someone who understands that money is not just mathematical, but emotional, psychological, spiritual, and behavioral. If you haven't read his book The Life Progression System, I would suggest you stop here and go and read it first.

What makes this work powerful is its simplicity without shallowness. The GPS framework—location, destination, route, mode of travel, resources, and ETA—takes complex financial concepts and turns them into a navigable journey. You don't just read this book—you *travel through it.*

This is not a quick-fix guide. It is a **lifestyle system**. It doesn't promise instant wealth, but it does promise clarity, control, and confidence—three things most people have never had with money. It teaches readers how to eliminate debt, build credit, increase income, protect assets, and create legacy—all while maintaining peace.

Perhaps most importantly, this book restores **hope with structure**. It reminds readers that financial freedom is not reserved for the elite—it is available to the disciplined, the intentional, and the teachable.

If you follow the system in these pages, you will not only change your finances—you will change how you make decisions for the rest of your life.

That is real wealth.

AUTHOR'S NOTE

This book was not written to impress you. It was written to **walk with you**.

I want you to know something from the very beginning: I did not write *The Financial Progression System* from a place of perfection. I wrote it from a place of **experience, observation, correction, and calling**. I've seen what financial confusion does to families, marriages, mental health, faith, and future generations. I've also seen what clarity, structure, and discipline can do when people are finally given a system that makes sense.

This book exists because too many hardworking people were never taught how money actually works. Not in school. Not at home. And often—not even in spaces of faith where stewardship is preached but strategy is missing. I believe ignorance is not the issue—**lack of navigation is**. People don't fail financially because they don't care. They fail because they don't know where they are, where they're going, or how to get there.

That is why I wrote The Life Progression System and this book is written as the second step in the journey and not just a lesson.

You may find yourself nodding while reading certain sections. You may feel challenged in others. You may even feel exposed at times—and that's okay. Growth often begins with discomfort, but it never ends there. If you read this book honestly and apply it consistently, you will not only change your finances—you will change how you make decisions, how you manage pressure, and how you prepare for the future.

Please understand this: **this book is not meant to replace action**. It is meant to ignite it. Read it slowly. Revisit chapters. Take notes. Pause and implement. Progress is not about speed—it's about direction and follow-through.

And when you're ready to go deeper—when you want accountability, structure, and guided execution—know that this system extends beyond these pages. *The Financial Progression System* was designed to live, breathe, and evolve through continued education and community. Whether through future books, trainings, or structured programs like the Debt Eliminator offered through Savings Solutions, the goal remains the same: **to help you move from financial survival to financial sovereignty**.

Most importantly, remember this:
You are not broken.
You are not behind.
You are not incapable.

You were simply never given a map.

Now you have one!

Move forward with confidence.
Move forward with wisdom.
Move forward on purpose.

— **Rev. Darryl Bass**

Table of Contents

INTRODUCTION: Why Most People Stay Lost Financially

Why Hard Work Alone Doesn't Create Wealth

Most people were taught a simple formula for success: work hard, stay loyal, and everything will eventually work out. While hard work is honorable and necessary, it is not a wealth strategy. Millions of people work long hours every day and still remain financially strained, stressed, and stuck. Hard work produces income, but without structure, direction, and strategy, income alone rarely produces wealth. In fact, without a system, higher income often leads to higher expenses, not financial freedom.

Wealth is not created by effort alone—it is created by **intentional movement**. Two people can earn the same income and end up in completely different financial positions based on decisions, habits, and systems. One may build assets, savings, and security, while the other lives paycheck to paycheck. The difference is not work ethic; it is **financial navigation**. Without knowing where your money is going or why, hard work becomes motion without progress.

The Danger of Moving Without Direction

Movement feels productive, but movement without direction often leads in circles. Many people are "doing something" with their money—paying bills, making minimum payments, chasing side hustles—yet still feel like they are going nowhere. This creates frustration, exhaustion, and eventually hopelessness. When money decisions are reactive instead of strategic, progress becomes accidental rather than intentional.

Moving without direction financially is like driving without a destination. You may burn gas, put miles on the vehicle, and feel busy, but you are not actually getting closer to where you want to be. Without clarity, people make emotional decisions—spending to cope, borrowing to survive, and delaying planning because it feels overwhelming. Direction turns effort into progress; without it, even good intentions produce poor results.

Money Confusion vs. Money Clarity

Money confusion is one of the most common and damaging financial conditions today. It shows up as avoidance, anxiety, and inconsistency. People don't look at their numbers because they feel ashamed, overwhelmed, or afraid of what they'll find. This confusion creates paralysis—when you don't understand your money, you stop managing it, and when you stop managing it, it manages you.

Money clarity, on the other hand, brings peace—even before the money improves. Clarity doesn't require perfection; it requires honesty. When you understand where you are, what you owe, what you earn, and what you want, decisions become simpler and less emotional. Clarity replaces fear with focus. It allows you to move forward confidently because you are no longer guessing—you are navigating.

Introducing FPS: A Financial GPS for Real Life

The Financial Progression System (FPS) was created to give people what they were never taught: a **step-by-step navigation system for money**. Just like a GPS helps you get from your current location to a chosen destination, FPS helps you move from financial confusion to financial clarity, stability, and freedom. It does not judge where you start; it simply requires honesty about where you are.

FPS works because it follows a proven sequence: identify your current financial location, choose a clear destination, develop the best route, account for obstacles, and adjust as needed. Life is unpredictable, but progress does not have to be. FPS is not theory—it is a practical system designed for real people with real responsibilities, real setbacks, and real goals.

How FPS Differs from Budgeting, Hustle Culture, and Quick Fixes

Traditional budgeting often fails because it focuses only on restriction, not direction. Budgets tell you what you can't do, but they rarely explain why you're doing it or where you're headed. Hustle culture promises freedom through exhaustion, teaching people to work more instead of work smarter. Quick fixes offer temporary relief—consolidation loans, gimmicks, or shortcuts—without addressing behavior, mindset, or long-term sustainability.

FPS is different because it is **progression-based, not pressure-based**. It integrates mindset, strategy, systems, and accountability. It doesn't promise overnight success; it promises predictable progress. FPS teaches you how to think about money, how to move money, and how to build systems that continue working long after motivation fades. This is not about getting rich quick—it's about **never being lost again**.

This book is your map.
The system is your guide.
And your destination is no longer a mystery.

PART I — THE FINANCIAL PRE-TRIP INSPECTION

Before you move a dollar, you must inspect the driver.

Most people think their money is the problem. But money is rarely the first problem—it's usually the **mirror**. It reflects what we believe, what we fear, what we prioritize, and what we were trained to do long before we ever earned our first paycheck. That's why the Financial Progression System reiterates what the Life Progression System teaches and starts where most financial books refuse to start: **with the driver**.

Because if the driver is anxious, impulsive, ashamed, distracted, or convinced that "this is just how life is," it doesn't matter how good the plan is. The plan will be sabotaged on the road. So before we calculate, cut, invest, or save—we inspect. Not your bank account first. **Your mindset first.**

Chapter 1: Your Financial Mindset Check

Money Beliefs Formed in Childhood

The first time you learned about money wasn't in a classroom—it was in a living room, a kitchen, a car ride, or a stressful argument you weren't supposed to hear. Money beliefs are often "caught," not taught. You watched how the adults in your life responded to bills, setbacks, and prosperity. You heard phrases like, "We can't afford that," "Money doesn't grow on trees," "Rich people are greedy," or "When I get paid, I'm buying something for me." Those statements may sound normal, but they plant seeds—and those seeds grow into spending habits, fear patterns, and financial decisions that follow people into adulthood like a shadow.

Some households raised children to believe money was always scarce, always stressful, always out of reach. Others taught that money was a tool—something to plan with, build with, and steward. The problem is most people never stop to question which belief system they inherited. They simply live it out automatically. That is why two adults with the same income can have completely different outcomes—because their **financial programming** is different.

Here's the truth that frees you: inherited beliefs do not have to become permanent identities. What you learned is real, but it isn't necessarily true. If you were raised around financial struggle, that struggle may have trained you to make decisions based on survival instead of strategy. Survival decisions feel urgent, emotional, and "right now." Strategy decisions feel calm, clear, and "long-term." This chapter is where you begin shifting from inherited survival to intentional strategy.

The Deeper Root: Life Before Money

Before you can master money, you must master yourself.

Financial mindset is not isolated. It is connected to identity, discipline, emotional maturity, vision, faith, and personal responsibility. That is why this book focuses on financial progression — but it does not exist in isolation from personal progression.

If your life lacks structure, your money will lack structure. If your thinking lacks clarity, your spending will lack clarity. If your identity is unstable, your financial decisions will be inconsistent.

This is why I wrote *The Life Progression System.*

The Life Progression System addresses the internal architecture that supports every external outcome — discipline, time management, emotional regulation, purpose alignment, and long-term vision. Financial growth rests on that foundation.

Many people attempt to fix money without fixing habits. They attempt to build wealth without building structure. They try to create financial peace while living mentally scattered. That approach always collapses.

The Life Progression System teaches how to:

- Build daily structure
- Develop disciplined identity
- Strengthen decision-making
- Increase personal responsibility
- Align behavior with long-term vision

And once those are in place, financial mastery becomes sustainable.

If you find yourself repeatedly starting and stopping financially…
If you struggle more with consistency than knowledge…
If your money problems seem tied to deeper life patterns…

Then reading The Life Progression System before this book will strengthen the foundation beneath your financial journey.

Because financial progression is a branch.

Life progression is the root.

And roots determine fruit.

And yes, faith belongs here—not as pressure, but as perspective. Scripture reminds us that transformation happens from the inside out: *"Be transformed by the renewing of your mind…"* (Romans 12:2). That includes the part of your mind that thinks about money. Because once your mind changes, your behavior starts to follow—and when behavior changes consistently, outcomes change permanently.

Scarcity vs. Stewardship Thinking

Scarcity thinking says, "There's never enough." It makes you feel like life is a constant emergency. When scarcity is driving, even small problems feel like disasters. A flat tire becomes a crisis. A surprise bill becomes a panic attack. Scarcity thinking doesn't just limit your bank account—it limits your imagination. It convinces you that your best days are behind you, your options are few, and your financial story is already written. This is experience speaking, not theory thinking, I have lived it and I know what it will do.

The hidden danger of scarcity is that it creates self-fulfilling cycles. When you believe money is always leaving, you're more likely to hold onto it tightly or spend it impulsively—both of which block progress. Some people hoard out of fear. Others splurge because they assume they'll never get ahead anyway. Either way, scarcity keeps people stuck in reaction mode.

Stewardship thinking is different. Stewardship says, "I'm responsible for what flows through my hands." It doesn't deny reality—it just refuses to be ruled by it. Stewardship thinking understands that money is a tool, not a master. It teaches you to plan, prioritize, and make decisions with wisdom instead of emotion. Stewardship creates peace because it turns random financial chaos into intentional financial order.

The Bible captures this balance without turning money into an idol: *"The plans of the diligent lead surely to abundance…"* (Proverbs 21:5). Notice it doesn't say the wishes of the hopeful. It says the **plans** of the diligent. Stewardship is planning with discipline. And the moment you adopt stewardship, you stop feeling like money is happening *to you* and start realizing money can be directed *by you.*

Emotional Money Habits

Most financial problems don't start in your wallet—they start in your emotions. People don't overspend because they're "bad with money." They overspend because it gives temporary relief. A stressful day turns into a "I deserve this." Loneliness turns into online shopping. Anxiety turns into eating out. Depression turns into "let me treat myself." And the craziest part? The purchase often feels like victory—until the bank alert hits and the guilt shows up.

Emotional money habits are powerful because they are reinforced in the brain. Spending can release short-term pleasure. That's why people can know better and still do it. This is not about intelligence; it's about wiring. The habit is not just financial—it's neurological and emotional. That's why budgeting alone doesn't fix it. A budget can tell you what you *should* do, but your emotions will still pull you toward what feels good in the moment.

To break emotional money habits, you don't just need restraint—you need replacement. You need to identify the trigger, the behavior, and the payoff. Trigger: stress. Behavior: shopping. Payoff: relief. Then you replace the behavior with something that still gives relief without draining your future. That could be exercise, prayer, journaling, a walk, a phone call, or even a structured "fun fund" that allows enjoyment without destruction.

Scripture speaks to this principle of internal leadership: *"Above all else, guard your heart, for everything you do flows from it."* (Proverbs 4:23). Your spending flows from your heart. Your saving flows from your heart. Your discipline flows from your heart. Once you learn to manage what's happening inside of you, what happens in your bank account begins to change.

Why Mindset Determines Financial Outcomes

Your mindset is not a motivational phrase—it is a decision-making engine. It determines what you do with money when nobody is watching. It determines whether you track your spending or avoid it. Whether you pay extra on debt or make excuses. Whether you prepare for emergencies or pretend emergencies won't come. Your mindset is the invisible hand behind every visible financial outcome.

Before we move forward, let's pause and take inventory of our mindset.

Do This Now: Mindset Inventory

Step 1 — Childhood Money Messages
Write 10 phrases you heard growing up about money:

1. ____________________
2. ____________________
3. ____________________
4. ____________________
5. ____________________
6. ____________________
7. ____________________
8. ____________________
9. ____________________
10. ____________________

Step 2 — Classify each message
Label each phrase:

- **S** = Scarcity message (fear-based)
- **ST** = Stewardship message (wisdom-based)

Count them. _______
Which one dominates? ☐ **S** ☐ **ST**

That dominance still influences your decisions today.

Step 3 — Your current default
Finish these:

When I'm stressed, I tend to ____________ (spend / avoid / hoard / borrow).

When I get extra money, I usually ________________ (spend it / save it / invest it / payoff debt with it).

My biggest money emotion is ________ (fear / guilt / shame / pride / anxiety).

Step 4 — Rewrite your money belief
Choose the top 3 scarcity beliefs and rewrite them as stewardship truths:

Old belief:

1. ____
2. ____
3. ____

New stewardship truth:

1. ____

2. ____

3. ____

Checkpoint: You have identified your financial programming.

Scarcity thinking says:
"There's never enough."

Stewardship thinking says:
"I am responsible for what flows through my hands."

You cannot build wealth from scarcity.
You can only survive from it.

This is why so many people "make more" and still stay stuck. A bigger shovel doesn't fix a hole if you keep digging in the wrong direction. Without mindset change, people repeat patterns at higher levels: higher income, higher spending. New job, new car note. Better salary, bigger lifestyle. The result is the same stress—just with more zeros.

Mindset also determines how you respond to setbacks. When life hits you—and life will hit you—your mindset decides whether you quit or reroute. A debt-free journey isn't a straight line. It's a route with detours, construction zones, and unexpected delays. People with a weak mindset interpret setbacks as proof they can't win. People with a trained mindset interpret setbacks as signals to adjust. That one difference decides whether you stay in bondage or break through.

Here's the dopamine truth: when your mindset is aligned, progress becomes addictive. You start craving results. You start wanting to check your balances because it feels like winning. You start enjoying saying no because it proves you're in control. You stop needing motivation because discipline starts producing evidence—and evidence fuels belief. You don't just hope you'll be debt-free. You start feeling it in your behavior.

And that's the shift. Because FPS is not just about money—it's about mastery.

Now that you've inspected the driver, you're ready for the next part of the pre-trip inspection: the moment you stop guessing and start seeing clearly. In the next chapter, we're going to expose what most people never identify until it's too late—**financial trauma patterns** and the hidden behaviors they produce. Because once you can name the pattern, you can break it.

You're not just learning about money anymore. You're reclaiming control.

Chapter 2: Financial Trauma & Money Behaviors

How unresolved pain silently controls money—and how to take that control back.

Financial trauma does not announce itself loudly. It shows up quietly in habits we normalize, excuse, or avoid altogether. Many people believe their financial struggles are caused by math, income, or bad luck, when in reality the root issue is emotional conditioning. Trauma teaches the nervous system how to respond long before logic ever gets a chance to speak. Until that conditioning is addressed, even the best financial plans will be undermined.

Do This Now: "Trigger → Behavior → Replacement" Worksheet

Step 1 — Identify your top 5 triggers

Examples: stress, loneliness, boredom, family pressure, payday excitement.

Write yours:

	Trigger	Behavior	Replacement
ex	*Bonus check*	*Buy something*	*Invest in something*
1.			
2.			
3.			
4.			
5.			

Step 2 — Identify the behavior
What do you usually do when that trigger hits?

1. Buy something
2. Eat out
3. Ignore bills
4. Apply for credit
5. Say "I'll fix it later"

Write the behavior number next to each trigger or write your own.

Step 3 — Replace (not just resist)
For each trigger, choose a replacement action that still gives relief, but doesn't drain your future:

1. Walk/prayer
2. Journal
3. 10-minute cleanup
4. Call accountability partner
5. "Fun fund" spending cap

Write the replacement number next to each trigger or write your own.

Checkpoint: You have a plan to break emotional money cycles.

This chapter exists to pull back the curtain. Not to shame you—but to **free you**. Once you can identify the behavior, you can interrupt it. Once you can name the pattern, you can rewrite it. And once you understand that healing must come before building, progress stops being painful and starts becoming powerful.

Spending as Coping

For many people, spending is not about things—it's about relief. After a long day, a stressful conversation, or an emotional low point, spending provides a temporary sense of control, pleasure, or reward. The purchase feels like a win in the moment, a way to reclaim joy or autonomy. This is why emotional spending often happens even when someone knows better. Logic loses to emotion when emotion is unaddressed.

The brain rewards this behavior chemically. Spending triggers dopamine, the same neurotransmitter associated with pleasure and motivation. Over time, the brain learns that stress + spending = relief. This creates a loop, not a strategy. The problem is that dopamine fades quickly, while the financial consequence remains. Guilt replaces pleasure, stress increases, and the cycle repeats—stronger than before.

Scripture reminds us that unmanaged emotion can lead us astray: *"Whoever has no rule over his own spirit is like a city broken down, without walls."* (Proverbs 25:28). Emotional spending is not a money issue—it's a boundary issue. Healing begins when spending is no longer used as medicine and emotional regulation is addressed at the source. When that happens, money stops being an escape and becomes the tool it should be.

Fear-Based Saving and Hoarding

While some people cope by spending, others cope by gripping tightly. Fear-based saving looks responsible on the surface, but underneath it is anxiety, distrust, and a constant expectation of loss. These individuals save—not from peace—but from fear. They are afraid to invest, afraid to enjoy, afraid to move forward because they believe security can disappear at any moment.

This behavior often develops in people who experienced instability: inconsistent income, sudden loss, or financial betrayal. Hoarding money becomes a way to feel safe, but safety without movement leads to stagnation. Money that is never deployed intentionally eventually becomes another form of emotional prison—one built on "what if" scenarios instead of wisdom.

Jesus addressed this mindset gently but clearly: *"For where your treasure is, there your heart will be also."* (Matthew 6:21). When fear guards money, money guards the heart. True financial peace is not found in hoarding—it is found in **stewardship**, where saving, giving, and investing all have purpose. Healing fear-based saving means learning to trust systems, planning, and God's provision rather than relying solely on accumulation.

Avoidance, Denial, and Procrastination

One of the most common trauma responses is avoidance. People don't check balances. They don't open mail. They delay decisions. They say, "I'll deal with it later," not because they don't care—but because caring feels overwhelming. Avoidance is the nervous system saying, "I can't handle this right now."

Denial protects emotions in the short term but destroys progress in the long term. Bills don't disappear because we ignore them. Interest doesn't pause because we delay. Avoidance allows problems to compound quietly, often until a crisis forces action. By then, stress is higher, options are fewer, and shame is heavier.

Scripture gives wisdom without condemnation: *"The simple believe anything, but the prudent give thought to their steps."* (Proverbs

14:15). Avoidance keeps people stuck reacting instead of choosing. Healing avoidance starts with small, consistent exposure—looking, tracking, acknowledging—without judgment. Progress begins the moment fear stops deciding what gets attention.

Healing Before Building

This is one of the most important principles in the entire Financial Progression System: **you cannot build wealth on unhealed behavior.** It's like building a mansion on sinking sand, it will soon be devoured. Many people try to jump straight into budgets, investments, and income strategies without addressing the emotional foundation. The result is frustration, inconsistency, and eventual burnout. Systems fail when the person using them is still in survival mode.

Healing does not mean waiting until you "feel ready." It means acknowledging the patterns that sabotage progress and committing to growth alongside strategy. When healing comes first, building becomes sustainable. Discipline stops feeling like punishment and starts feeling like self-respect. Planning stops feeling restrictive and starts feeling empowering.

The Bible reflects this order clearly: *"A wise man builds his house on the rock."* (Matthew 7:24). Healing is the rock. Without it, every financial storm will knock the structure down. With it, progress becomes resilient. FPS is designed to help you heal **while** you build—so momentum feels safe, progress feels exciting, and freedom becomes inevitable.

Now that you understand how trauma shapes behavior, it's time to strengthen the part of you that makes daily decisions—the will. In the next chapter, we will focus on **willingness,**

discipline, and financial obedience, because awareness alone is not enough. Freedom requires follow-through.

You are no longer reacting.
You are preparing to lead.

Chapter 3: Willingness, Discipline, and Financial Obedience

Why knowing better is not the same as doing better—and how true change is sustained.

Information can inspire you. Motivation can excite you. But **only discipline can transform you**. This chapter is where the Financial Progression System shifts from awareness to action. Many people stall here—not because they lack knowledge, but because they underestimate the power of consistency. Willingness opens the door, discipline keeps you moving, and obedience ensures you arrive.

This chapter is about mastering the internal controls that govern your external outcomes. Because once your behavior aligns with your vision, progress becomes inevitable.

Why Information Without Discipline Fails

We live in the most informed generation in history—and one of the most financially stressed. People know about budgeting, credit scores, investing, and debt payoff strategies, yet still feel stuck. The problem isn't ignorance; it's inconsistency. Information tells you what to do. Discipline determines whether you actually do it—especially when it's inconvenient.

Discipline is what bridges the gap between intention and outcome. Without it, good plans remain ideas and strong starts end in frustration. This is why people bounce from book to book, program to program, hoping the next piece of information will finally "click." But information does not create change—**repetition does**.

Scripture reinforces this principle clearly: *"Do not merely listen to the word, and so deceive yourselves. Do what it says."* (James 1:22). Financial freedom works the same way. Hearing truth without applying it creates self-deception. Discipline is not about perfection; it's about follow-through. When discipline is present, progress compounds—even when motivation fades.

Do This Now: "Discipline System Setup"

Step 1 — Pick your daily money habit (only pick 1):
Choose one:

- ☐ Track spending 5 minutes/day
- ☐ Check balances daily
- ☐ No unplanned purchases
- ☐ Pack lunch 3x/week
- ☐ Pay $5–$25 extra on debt daily/weekly

Write your choice: ________

Step 2 — Build the "obedience rule"
Finish this sentence:

"Before I spend, I will ask: ______________________________."

Examples:

- "Does this align with my destination?"
- "Is this planned or emotional?"
- "What will this cost me in peace?"

Step 3 — 30-Day Progress Tracker
Check one for each day you obey the rule. Miss a day start over.

01	02	03	04	05	06	07	08	09	10
11	12	13	14	15	16	17	18	19	20
21	22	23	24	25	26	27	28	29	30

Financial Obedience vs. Impulse

Impulse is emotional, immediate, and reactive. Obedience is intentional, planned, and values-driven. Financial impulse says, "I want it now." Financial obedience asks, "Does this align with where I'm going?" One responds to feelings; the other responds to vision. And whichever one you practice more often becomes your default.

Impulse spending doesn't always feel reckless. Sometimes it feels justified — "I've worked hard," "I deserve this," or "I'll make it up later." But impulse decisions rarely consider long-term impact. Obedience does. Obedience is not about restriction—it's about **alignment**. It's choosing actions today that agree with the future you say you want.

The Bible frames obedience as protection, not punishment: *"If you are willing and obedient, you shall eat the good of the land."* (Isaiah 1:19). Financial obedience isn't about denying joy; it's about postponing lesser pleasures for greater peace. When obedience becomes habitual, impulse loses its power—and money starts moving with purpose instead of emotion.

Choosing Delayed Gratification

Delayed gratification is the muscle that separates financial survivors from financial builders. It is the ability to say no now so you can say yes later. This doesn't mean never enjoying life—it means enjoying life **without sabotaging your future**. Every financial decision is a trade-off between present comfort and future stability.

The challenge is that delayed gratification doesn't feel rewarding at first. There's no applause for skipping a purchase.

No celebration for making an extra debt payment. But beneath the surface, something powerful is happening—**confidence is being built**. Each disciplined choice proves to your brain that you are in control, and control is deeply rewarding over time.

Scripture reminds us of this long view: *"Better is the end of a thing than the beginning thereof."* (Ecclesiastes 7:8). Delayed gratification trains you to value outcomes over urges. Eventually, progress itself becomes the reward. Watching balances drop, savings grow, and stress decrease releases a deeper, longer-lasting sense of satisfaction than any impulse buy ever could.

The Dopamine Shift: From Spending to Progress

Here's the breakthrough most people don't expect: discipline eventually becomes pleasurable. As progress becomes visible, dopamine stops coming from spending and starts coming from **winning**. You begin to crave results. Tracking feels empowering. Saying no feels strong. Following the plan feels like momentum.

This is where obedience stops feeling like sacrifice and starts feeling like identity. You're no longer "trying to be disciplined"—you *are* disciplined. And once discipline becomes identity, relapse becomes rare and progress becomes normal.

You now understand that willingness opens the door, discipline moves you forward, and obedience keeps you aligned. With the driver inspected, healed, and trained, it's finally time to look at the dashboard.

In the next part of the Financial Progression System, we move from internal readiness to external reality—**determining your financial starting point**. No more guessing. No more assumptions. Just clarity.

You are no longer hoping for change.
You are prepared to execute it.

PART II — DETERMINING YOUR STARTING POINT

The GPS cannot guide what you refuse to locate.

You can't navigate from denial. You can't build from assumptions. And you can't reach financial freedom with foggy numbers and hopeful thinking. This is the part of the Financial Progression System where everything becomes real—in the best way. Because clarity is not condemnation. Clarity is **control**.

Most people avoid this step because they think looking will hurt. But what actually hurts us is **not looking**—because what you don't measure, you can't manage, and what you can't manage eventually masters you. In this chapter, you're going to locate your financial position with precision, not panic. You're going to replace emotion with evidence, and you're going to start feeling the kind of momentum that makes you want to keep going—because progress becomes addictive once you can see it.

Chapter 4: Locating Your Financial Position

Net Worth vs. Self-Worth

One of the biggest reasons people avoid checking their financial position is because they tie their finances to their identity. They don't just think, "My numbers are low." They think, "I'm behind." They don't just see debt—they feel shame. They don't just see missed payments—they feel like a failure. That's why we start here with a critical separation: **your net worth is a number; your self-worth is a God-given reality.**

Your net worth is simply a snapshot of your financial life today. It's the difference between what you own and what you owe. It may reflect choices, circumstances, and seasons—but it does not define your value. Your self-worth is not calculated by credit scores, income, or what you can afford. If you confuse net worth with self-worth, you will avoid the truth to protect your emotions. And when you avoid the truth, you delay transformation.

This is where the enemy wins quietly: not through your numbers, but through your interpretation of them. The goal of this chapter is to teach you to look at numbers without flinching. To see the truth without shame. To treat your financial position like a dashboard—not a verdict. Your car's dashboard isn't there to insult you; it's there to inform you. If the gas light is on, that doesn't mean the car is "bad." It means it needs attention.

Scripture reinforces this foundation without heaviness: *"As a man thinks in his heart, so is he."* (Proverbs 23:7). If you think your value rises and falls with your finances, you will live emotionally chained to money. But once you separate identity from inventory, you gain the power to make decisions from peace instead of pain. And peace is the environment where progress grows best.

Income, Expenses, Assets, Liabilities

To locate your financial position, you don't need a finance degree—you need a clear structure. Think of this as the "You Are Here" dot on a map. Four categories create the map: **income, expenses, assets, and liabilities.** When you understand these four areas, confusion begins to disappear because you can finally see what's happening instead of guessing.

Income is every dollar coming in—paychecks, side gigs, business revenue, benefits, child support, and any recurring deposits. Most people know their income roughly, but not precisely. Precision matters because your plan will only be as accurate as your numbers. If you overestimate income or forget irregular income, you'll build a plan that collapses under reality.

Expenses are every dollar going out—bills, subscriptions, groceries, eating out, gas, entertainment, and all the silent leaks people forget about. Expenses are where the truth often surprises people. Not because they're reckless, but because spending becomes automatic. That's why the first "dopamine hit" in this chapter is powerful: the moment you identify leaks, you realize you can redirect money immediately without making more money. That's when hope becomes tangible.

Assets are what you own that has value—cash, savings, retirement accounts, vehicles, property, investments, and even business equipment. **Liabilities** are what you owe—credit cards, personal loans, auto loans, student loans, medical bills, collections, and mortgages. This isn't about labeling yourself. It's about labeling reality so you can move strategically. The moment you put everything in the right category, you stop feeling "lost" and start feeling like a builder standing over blueprints.

Scripture points to the power of clear accounting without turning it into anxiety: *"Suppose one of you wants to build a tower. Won't you first sit down and estimate the cost…?"* (Luke 14:28). Estimating cost is not fear. It's wisdom. And wisdom is what turns financial struggle into financial strategy.

Why Numbers Tell the Truth Without Judgment

Numbers are honest, but they are not hostile. They don't shame you. They don't accuse you. They don't bring up your past. Numbers simply report what is. And that's why they are powerful—they remove the drama and replace it with direction. When you finally see your true financial position, you gain something priceless: **certainty**.

Most fear around money comes from uncertainty. "I think I'm behind." "I feel like I can't catch up." "I don't know where it's going." But when you put the numbers on paper, uncertainty loses its power. You don't have to guess. You don't have to assume. You don't have to fear imaginary worst-case scenarios. You can look at the truth and say, "Now I know—and because I know, I can move."

This is the moment many people experience a surprising emotional shift: relief. Even if the numbers aren't ideal, the clarity is calming. Because clarity gives control, and control reduces anxiety. The brain relaxes when it understands the problem. Confusion creates stress; clarity creates stability.

Numbers also create measurable progress, which spikes dopamine in a healthy way. When you know your starting point, you can track improvement. Debt dropping by $200 is no longer "small"—it's visible progress. Savings growing to $500 is no longer "nothing"—it's a milestone. Credit score increases by 25 points are no longer "random"—they're results. The numbers become proof that you are changing your life.

Scripture supports this concept of honest measurement and steady progress: *"Let us examine our ways and test them, and let us return to the Lord."* (Lamentations 3:40). Examination isn't condemnation—it's correction. It's the beginning of renewal. And in financial terms, it's the beginning of momentum.

How to Complete Your Personal Net Worth Statement

A Step-by-Step Financial Clarity Walkthrough

Before you begin, understand this: your net worth is not a judgment. It is a measurement. Numbers do not define your value; they reveal your starting point. You cannot improve what you refuse to measure. This exercise is about awareness, not shame.

Step 1: Choose Your Date

At the top of the form, write today's date. A net worth statement is a snapshot in time. This gives you a benchmark to compare progress in the future.

Prepared for is you!

Step 2: List Your Assets — What You Own

Assets are everything of financial value that belongs to you.

Start with liquid assets:
Add up balances in your checking and savings accounts. Use real numbers from current statements, not estimates.

Move to investments:
List retirement accounts, brokerage accounts, stocks, and any ownership in a business. Use current market values.

Next, real estate:
Write the current estimated market value of your home or properties. Do not subtract the mortgage yet. That comes later.

Then personal property:
Include vehicles at their current resale value, not what you paid for them.

When finished, total everything in this section. This is your Total Assets number.

Statement Date:	
Prepared For:	
SECTION I — ASSETS (What You Own)	
Liquid Assets	
Checking Accounts	

Total Checking Accounts	
Savings Accounts	
Total Savings Accounts	
Cash on Hand	
Money Market / CDs	
Total Money Market / CDs	
Total Liquid Assets	**$**
Investment Assets	
401(k) / 403(b)	
Total 401(k) / 403(b)	
IRA / Roth IRA	
Total IRA / Roth IRA	
Brokerage Accounts	
Total Brokerage Accounts	
Stocks / Bonds / Mutual Funds	

Total Stocks / Bonds / Mutual Funds	
Business Ownership Interest	
Total Business Ownership Interest	
Total Investment Assets	**$0**
Real Estate Assets	
Primary Residence (Market Value)	
Rental Property #1	
Rental Property #2	
Land / Other Real Estate	
Total Real Estate Assets	$
Personal & Other Assets	
Vehicles (Market Value)	
Total Vehicles (Market Value)	
Life Insurance (Cash Value Only)	

Total Life Insurance (Cash Value Only)	
Valuable Property	
Intellectual Property	
Total Intellectual Property	
Other Assets	
Total Personal & Other Assets	**$**
TOTAL ASSETS	**$0**

Step 3: List Your Liabilities — What You Owe

Liabilities are debts and financial obligations.

Start with secured debts:
Mortgage balances and auto loans. Use remaining balances.

Then unsecured debts:
Credit cards, student loans, personal loans, medical debt.

Include any taxes owed or business obligations.

Add these together. This becomes your Total Liabilities.

SECTION II — LIABILITIES (What You Owe)	
Secured Debt	
Mortgage Balance	
Primary Residence Mortgage	
Rental Property #1 Mortgage	
Rental Property #2 Mortgage	

Land/Other Real Estate Mortgage	
Total Mortgage Balance	
Auto Loans	
Total Auto Loans	
Other Secured Loans	
Total Other Secured Loans	
Total Secured Debt	**$**
Unsecured Debt	
Credit Cards	
Total Credit Cards	
Student Loans	
Total Student Loans	
Personal Loans	

Total Personal Loans	
Medical Debt	
Total Medical Debt	
Other Unsecured Debt	
Total Other Unsecured Debt	
Total Unsecured Debt	**$0**
Other Liabilities	
Taxes Owed	
Total Taxes Owed	
Business Loans	
Total Business Loans	
Other Obligations	
Total Other Liabilities	**$0**
TOTAL LIABILITIES	**$0**

Step 4: Calculate Net Worth

Net Worth = Total Assets – Total Liabilities

If the number is positive, you are building wealth.
If it is negative, you are in a rebuilding phase.
Both are acceptable starting points. What matters is direction.

NET WORTH SUMMARY	
Total Assets	**$**
Total Liabilities	**$**
NET WORTH	**$**

Step 5: Reflect Strategically

Ask yourself:
Is most of my money working for me, or am I working for debt? ☐ Yes ☐ No

What is my largest liability? ______________________________.

What asset can I grow this year?

☐ Liquid Assets ☐ Investment Assets
☐ Real Estate Assets ☐ Personal & Other Assets

What debt can I eliminate first? __________________________.

Clarity creates strategy.

Step 6: Set a 12-Month Target

Write a realistic net worth goal for one year from now.
This could mean:
Reducing debt by a set amount
Increasing savings
Building investments
Increasing income

My 12-Month Net Worth Target: $________________

Then identify three concrete actions you will take immediately.

Three Strategic Actions to Improve This Number:

1. ____
2. ____
3. ____

Final Thought

Your net worth today is not your destiny.
It is your baseline.

Progression begins with truth.
Stability begins with structure.
Legacy begins with discipline.

Measure it.
Improve it.
Repeat quarterly.

Now that you've located your financial position, the next step is to dig deeper into what drives your daily reality: **cash flow**. Because debt payoff, saving, and wealth building don't begin with dreams—they begin with what's left over each month after life happens.

In the next chapter, you're going to learn how to identify where your money is flowing, where it's leaking, and how to create **instant financial breathing room**—often without making a single extra dollar.

You've found your location.
Now it's time to choose your direction—and start moving with confidence.

Chapter 5: Cash Flow Awareness

Because debt freedom isn't just about what you make—it's about what you keep and control.

Cash flow is the real heartbeat of your finances. It's not your salary, your credit score, or your intentions—it's the **movement** of money through your life every week and every month. Two people can earn the same income, and one feels financially suffocated while the other feels steady and empowered. The difference is rarely intelligence. It's cash flow awareness.

This chapter is where you stop asking, "Why am I always broke?" and start saying, "Now I see exactly what's happening." And once you can see it, you can control it. That's where momentum begins—because cash flow clarity doesn't just create progress, it creates *confidence.* Confidence becomes energy. Energy becomes consistency. And consistency becomes freedom.

Where Money Leaks

Most people don't "lose" money—they **leak** money. Leaks are small outflows that feel harmless in isolation, but destructive in combination. They are the forgotten subscriptions, the convenience spending, the "just this once" purchases that show up multiple times a week. Leaks don't feel like major decisions, which is why they're so dangerous. They slip under your radar and quietly steal your future.

A money leak is anything that pulls cash from your pocket without giving you real value, real progress, or real peace. It's not always something "bad"—it's often something unexamined. The coffee isn't the issue. The issue is the *pattern.*

The problem isn't eating out once. The problem is eating out so often that your financial goals can't breathe. Leaks thrive in busyness because busyness prevents tracking.

Here's how you identify leaks without confusion: you look for spending that is **frequent, emotional, and unplanned**. Frequent means it happens often. Emotional means it's tied to stress, boredom, reward, or comfort. Unplanned means it wasn't assigned a purpose before it happened. When you find spending that fits those three, you've likely found the leak. The good news? Leaks are fixable quickly—often within one week.

And here's the dopamine hit: every leak you plug becomes instant progress. It's like finding money you didn't know you had. When you redirect a $60 subscription stack, a $35 weekly convenience habit, or recurring fees you forgot existed, you immediately create cash flow that can go toward debt, savings, or stability. Scripture speaks to this principle simply: *"Whoever is faithful with little will be faithful with much."* (Luke 16:10). Plugging leaks is "little" that becomes "much" through consistency.

Fixed vs. Variable Expenses

If you don't understand the difference between fixed and variable expenses, you'll always feel confused about where your money went. **Fixed expenses** are predictable and usually consistent: rent/mortgage, car payment, insurance, minimum debt payments, tuition, and subscription services. They don't change much month to month, which means they are easier to plan for—but also harder to adjust quickly unless you restructure your lifestyle or renegotiate terms.

Variable expenses are flexible and often unpredictable: groceries, gas, eating out, entertainment, shopping, personal care, and hobbies. These are the categories where people either win or lose their cash flow. Variable expenses feel small, but they accumulate fast because they happen frequently. You don't typically go over budget on rent by accident, but you can absolutely go over budget on variable spending without realizing it.

Here's the key that eliminates uncertainty: fixed expenses determine your baseline survival, but variable expenses determine your freedom. If your variable spending is uncontrolled, your financial plan will always feel like it "should work" but doesn't. That's because variable expenses are where emotion and impulse often show up. Mastering variable expenses doesn't require suffering—it requires structure: categories, spending caps, and intentional choices.

A powerful strategy is to assign every variable dollar a job before the month begins. Groceries have a lane. Gas has a lane. Eating out has a lane. When you do this, spending becomes purposeful instead of random. Scripture supports intentionality without pressure: *"The plans of the diligent lead surely to abundance."* (Proverbs 21:5). Diligence isn't extreme—it's consistent planning. Once you plan your variable spending, cash flow becomes predictable, and predictability makes progress feel exciting instead of stressful.

Creating Your Personal Cash Flow Statement

Now that you understand where money leaks, and you clearly see the difference between fixed and variable expenses, it's time for a defining moment in this journey.

We are going to measure your financial heartbeat.

A cash flow statement answers one powerful question:

Is money flowing toward your freedom—or away from it?

This is not about judgment. It is about awareness. When you can see the movement of your money clearly, control becomes possible. And once control becomes possible, confidence follows.

Take a deep breath. Let's build this step-by-step.

Step 1: Identify Your Monthly Income

Write down every source of income you receive in a typical month.

Salary (after taxes)
Side income
Business income
Child support
Rental income
Any consistent deposits

Do not use your gross pay unless you are self-employed. Use what actually hits your bank account. This is your real working number.

Month:	
Prepared By:	
SECTION I — INCOME (Money Coming In After Taxes)	
Primary Employment Income	
Spouse Income	

Business Income	
Side Hustle Income	
Rental Income	
Child Support / Other Income	
Other Income	
TOTAL MONTHLY INCOME	**$0**

Add everything together.

This is your Total Monthly Income.

Now pause. This number represents your earning power. Respect it.

Step 2: List Your Fixed Expenses

Next, write down every fixed monthly obligation.

Rent or mortgage
Car payment
Insurance
Minimum debt payments
Phone
Internet
Subscriptions
Tuition

These are your baseline survival costs. They do not move much month to month.

SECTION II — FIXED EXPENSES (Baseline Survival Costs)	
Rent / Mortgage	
Property Taxes (if separate)	
Car Payment(s)	
Auto Insurance	
Health Insurance	
Life Insurance	
Utilities (Electric / Gas / Water)	
Phone	
Internet	
Subscriptions	
Minimum Debt Payments	
Tuition / Childcare	
Other Fixed Expenses	
TOTAL FIXED EXPENSES	**$0**

Add them together.

This is your Total Fixed Expenses.

Step 3: Calculate Your Variable Expenses

Now estimate your monthly average for:

Groceries
Gas
Eating out
Entertainment
Shopping
Personal care
Miscellaneous spending

If you're unsure, review the last 30 days of bank statements. Don't guess—verify.

SECTION III — VARIABLE EXPENSES (Flexible & Lifestyle Spending)	
Groceries	
Gas / Transportation	
Eating Out	
Entertainment	
Shopping	
Personal Care	
Household Supplies	
Miscellaneous	
TOTAL VARIABLE EXPENSES	**$0**

Add these together.

This is your Total Variable Expenses.

Step 4: Calculate Your Financial Position

Now let's do the math:

Total Income - Total Fixed Expenses - Total Variable Expenses = Net Cash Flow

SECTION IV — CASH FLOW SUMMARY	
Total Monthly Income	**$**
Minus Total Fixed Expenses	**$**
Minus Total Variable Expenses	**$**
NET CASH FLOW (Surplus or Deficit)	**$**

What remains?

If the number is positive, you have a surplus.
If the number is zero, you are breaking even.
If the number is negative, you have a deficit.

This is not good or bad. It is information.

And information is power.

Step 5: Interpret the Results

If you have a surplus, that surplus is your weapon. It is the fuel for debt elimination, savings growth, and investment.

If you are breaking even, your progress is being stalled by structure, not income. We refine structure.

If you are in deficit, now you understand why stress has been present. The math reveals the tension. But now that you see it, you can change it.

Clarity replaces confusion.
Structure replaces chaos.
Direction replaces frustration.

This is cash flow awareness.

And once you can see your financial heartbeat clearly, you are no longer drifting.

You are commanding.

Now that you know exactly how money moves through your life, we're ready for the next level of clarity—because understanding cash flow prepares you for something even more powerful: debt strategy.

You're not just managing money anymore.

You're building command over it.

The Silent Killers of Progress

Silent killers aren't always big bills. They're the subtle habits and hidden patterns that quietly suffocate your financial goals. One silent killer is **lifestyle inflation**—when your income increases and your expenses rise to match it. Many people get a raise but don't get ahead because new money gets assigned to new spending instead of debt reduction, savings, or investment. Progress dies quietly when upgrades become automatic.

Another silent killer is **minimum payments**. Minimum payments create the illusion of responsibility while stretching debt into long-term bondage. They keep you "current" but not "free." Interest works like a tax against your future, and if you only pay minimums, your money keeps working for lenders instead of for you. That's why cash flow awareness is essential—because every extra dollar you find becomes a weapon against interest.

A third silent killer is **financial neglect**—not checking accounts, not tracking spending, not reviewing subscriptions, not monitoring credit, and not managing due dates. Neglect isn't laziness—it's often overwhelm. But neglect compounds. Small issues become bigger problems. Fees stack. Balances grow. Opportunities are missed. The remedy isn't perfection; it's a weekly rhythm of attention.

And perhaps the most underestimated silent killer is **inconsistent focus**. People start strong, then get distracted, discouraged, or overly busy. Progress slows, and the brain interprets slow progress as failure. But slow progress isn't failure—it's still progress. That's why systems matter more than motivation. Scripture offers a steady encouragement here: *"Let us not grow weary in doing good, for in due season we shall reap, if we do not lose heart."* (Galatians 6:9). Cash flow mastery is "doing good" in small consistent ways until harvest shows up as debt freedom and financial peace.

Now that you can see where money leaks, understand fixed vs. variable spending, and recognize the silent killers of progress, you're ready for a major moment in the journey: **debt clarity**. Because you cannot defeat an enemy you refuse to measure.

In the next chapter, we'll create your full **Debt Inventory & Risk Exposure** profile—so you know exactly what you owe, where the danger is, which balances to attack first, and how to protect yourself while you eliminate debt.

You're not just managing money anymore.
You're building command over it.

Chapter 6: Debt Inventory & Risk Exposure

You cannot conquer what you refuse to identify—and you cannot eliminate what you misunderstand.

Debt is one of the most misunderstood tools in modern finance. For some, it feels normal. For others, it feels suffocating. But for most people, debt is confusing because it wears disguises. Some debt promises opportunity. Some debt quietly drains your future. And unless you learn how to tell the difference, debt will continue to control the pace and direction of your life.

This chapter is not about fear—it's about **clarity and authority**. When you understand your debt, you stop being intimidated by it. When you inventory it, you take away its power to surprise you. And when you understand risk exposure, you move from reaction to strategy. This chapter exists to turn debt from a vague burden into a **defined opponent**—one you can defeat.

Good Debt vs. Destructive Debt

Not all debt is created equal, but all debt carries responsibility. **Good debt** is often described as debt that has the potential to increase your income, net worth, or long-term stability. This is what I refer to as **Productive Debt**. Examples include certain education costs, income-producing real estate, or a business investment that generates positive cash flow. When structured correctly, good debt works *for* you instead of against you.

However, even "good debt" can become destructive if it is mismanaged. Over borrowing, poor timing, or unrealistic projections can turn opportunity into pressure. This is why good debt still requires discipline, planning, and risk awareness. Debt that produces growth must still fit within your cash flow and long-term vision—or it becomes another weight.

Destructive debt, on the other hand, is debt that consistently removes money from your future without producing value. High-interest credit cards, personal loans for lifestyle spending, payday loans, and financing depreciating items fall into this category. This is what I known as **Consumer Debt**. These debts don't build; they drain. They create stress, restrict options, and slow progress even when income increases.

Scripture speaks to this reality plainly: *"The borrower is servant to the lender."* (Proverbs 22:7). This verse isn't condemnation—it's caution. Debt creates obligation. The goal of FPS is not to shame debt, but to **reduce servitude and increase sovereignty**. Once you identify which debts are helping and which are harming, your strategy becomes clear—and clarity fuels momentum.

Consumer Debt vs. Productive Debt

Consumer debt and productive debt are not the same, even though both involve borrowing. Consumer debt is money borrowed to purchase items that decrease in value or do not generate income. Credit card balances for lifestyle purchases, retail financing, personal loans for vacations, and high-interest installment plans are common examples. Consumer debt typically drains future income because it requires repayment with interest while the purchased item often loses value quickly. It reduces flexibility, slows wealth building, and can create long-term financial pressure if not managed aggressively.

Productive debt, by contrast, is borrowing used to acquire assets or opportunities that have the potential to generate income or appreciate in value. Examples include real estate investments, business capital, or education strategically aligned with earning potential. The key difference is intention and return on investment. Productive debt is taken with a clear plan, defined payoff strategy, and measurable upside. It is structured, evaluated, and managed carefully rather than emotionally assumed.

The distinction is not about whether debt exists, but whether it builds or burdens. Consumer debt consumes tomorrow's income. Productive debt, when used wisely and conservatively, can accelerate income growth. The discipline lies in asking a simple question before borrowing:

Will this obligation increase my earning power or decrease my financial freedom? ☐ Yes ☐ No

That question alone separates reaction from strategy.

Interest as a Financial Predator

Interest is often presented as a neutral concept, but when misunderstood, it behaves like a predator—quiet, patient, and relentless. Interest doesn't rush. It compounds. It feeds on time, consistency, and inattention. And the longer it's ignored, the more powerful it becomes.

High-interest consumer debt is especially dangerous because it compounds daily or monthly while providing no return. Every dollar paid in interest is a dollar that cannot be saved, invested, or used to build stability. Over time, interest silently taxes your income and extends your dependence on lenders. This is why people feel like they're working harder but getting nowhere—interest is siphoning progress behind the scenes.

What makes interest predatory is that it disguises itself as manageable. The payments feel small. The statements look routine. But when you calculate the total cost over time, the truth becomes shocking. A purchase made for convenience today can cost two or three times its value tomorrow. That realization often triggers anger—but it should trigger **action**.

The Bible encourages wisdom around compounding forces, both positive and negative: *"The plans of the diligent lead surely to abundance."* (Proverbs 21:5). Compounding works both ways. Interest can destroy wealth—or, when reversed through investing and saving, it can build it. Eliminating high-interest debt is the fastest way to stop the bleeding and redirect compounding back in your favor.

The Minimum Payments Illusion

Minimum payments are one of the most dangerous illusions in personal finance. They create the appearance of responsibility while quietly extending bondage. Paying the minimum keeps you current—but it does not keep you progressing. In fact, minimum payments are designed to benefit lenders, not borrowers.

When you pay only the minimum, the majority of your payment often goes toward interest, not principal. This means you can pay faithfully for years and still owe almost the same balance. The illusion is subtle: statements praise you for being "on time," while the debt barely moves. This creates false confidence and delayed urgency.

Minimum payments also steal your cash flow. When balances linger, payments stay locked into your monthly budget, reducing flexibility and increasing stress. Emergencies feel heavier. Opportunities feel unreachable. Progress feels slow—not because you aren't trying, but because the system is working against you.

Scripture warns against slow traps that appear harmless: *"A little sleep, a little slumber… and poverty will come on you like a thief."* (Proverbs 6:10–11). Minimum payments operate the same way—slow, quiet, and deceptive. The solution isn't panic; it's **strategy**. When you move from minimum payments to intentional payoff plans, momentum returns quickly—and that momentum is deeply motivating.

Turning Inventory into Power

Here's the dopamine shift most people don't expect: once you fully inventory your debt—balances, interest rates, minimums, and risks—you stop feeling afraid and start feeling **focused**. Fear thrives in vagueness. Confidence grows in clarity. The moment debt becomes measurable, it becomes beatable.

Exercise: Turning Inventory into Power

From Fear to Focus in 30 Minutes

This is not a shame session.
This is a strategy session.
You are not your balances. You are the one eliminating them.

Step 1: Gather the Facts

Pull out:

- All credit card statements
- Loan statements
- Student loan balances
- Auto loan balances
- Personal loans
- Any money owed to individuals

No guessing. No estimating. Real numbers only.

Fear lives in approximation. Power lives in precision.

Step 2: Debt Inventory Table

On the next page you will find the Debt Inventory Worksheet, it is a simple form to complete, on each line you will put the following information in the appropriate column:

1. Creditor name
2. Total Balance
3. Interest Rate
4. Minimum Payment
5. Risk Level

Risk Level can be determined by:

High Risk – High interest rate, variable rate, or delinquent
Medium Risk – Moderate rate but large balance
Low Risk – Lower rate and stable

Debt Inventory Worksheet

Clarity Creates Power. Measurement Creates Momentum.

Name: ______________________________

Date:______________________________

Debt Inventory Table

Creditor	Total Balance	Interest Rate (%)	Minimum Payment	Risk Level

Step 3: Calculate the Total Debt Number

Add every balance together.

Total Debt: $____________________________

Pause.

That number is no longer a monster.
It is a target.

Step 4: Calculate Total Minimum Payments

Add every minimum payment together.

Total Monthly Minimum Payments: $__________________

Now ask:

How much of my monthly income is being consumed by minimums?

This reveals the choke point.

Step 5: Identify the First Target

Which debt is the most destructive?
Which one drains the most through interest?
Which one would give me momentum if eliminated?

Primary Target Debt: ___________________________

Why this is the first target: __________________________

One target creates focus.

Step 6: The Dopamine Shift

Write this down on a sheet of paper:

"I no longer fear my debt. I understand it. And what I understand, I can eliminate."

This is where the emotional shift happens.

Clarity removes vagueness.
Measurement removes imagination.
Strategy replaces fear.

This forces strategic thinking instead of emotional thinking.

Debt inventory is not about labeling yourself—it's about labeling reality so you can dismantle it. When you see which debts are destructive, which interest rates are draining you, and how minimum payments are slowing you down, the path forward becomes obvious. And when the path is obvious, action feels exciting instead of overwhelming.

Now that you understand your debt and risk exposure, it's time to examine the invisible force that lenders judge before they ever approve you: **your credit profile**. Because credit is not just a number—it's a financial reputation.

In the next chapter, we will uncover how credit works, why it matters, and how to regain control of it strategically—without obsession or fear.

You're no longer surrounded by debt.
You're preparing to dismantle it—
systematically.

Chapter 7: Credit Score & Financial Reputation

Credit isn't just a number—it's a report card of trust, and trust opens doors.

For many people, credit feels mysterious, stressful, or even insulting—like a number that judges your life. But credit was never designed to measure your worth as a human being. It measures something far more specific: **risk and reliability**. In other words, it's a financial reputation system—one that follows you into car purchases, home approvals, insurance pricing, business funding, and sometimes even employment decisions.

Here's the empowering truth: your credit score is not a permanent sentence. It is a **living result**—and anything that produces a result can be adjusted. This chapter will take the fog away. You will understand what credit really is, what your score is actually saying, and why the system seems to "see" things you overlook. The goal is not to obsess over credit—it's to master it so it stops mastering you.

Credit as Trust, Not Status

Credit is not a trophy. It's not a flex. It's not a social badge. Credit is simply a measurement of how much a lender believes they can trust you to pay back what you borrow—on time and as agreed. That's why credit is less about wealth and more about **behavior**. You can be high-income with poor credit, and you can be middle-income with excellent credit. Credit is not about how much you make; it's about how you manage obligations.

When you view credit as status, you either chase it for pride or avoid it because of shame. Both are traps. Status thinking creates obsession and comparison. Trust thinking creates clarity and strategy. You stop asking, "How do I look?" and start asking, "How do I build reliability?" That shift changes the way you use credit cards, loans, payments, and debt payoff plans.

Credit as trust also reframes the goal. The goal isn't "perfect credit." The goal is **better access** to opportunities with lower cost. Good credit reduces interest rates, increases approval odds, and expands options. It's not about looking impressive—it's about protecting your cash flow. Every point improvement can save you real money over time.

Scripture consistently teaches the power of a good name and trustworthy stewardship: *"A good name is to be chosen rather than great riches."* (Proverbs 22:1). In modern financial terms, your credit profile functions like a "name" in the marketplace. It's your reputation with institutions. And when your reputation is strong, doors open faster, cheaper, and with less stress.

What Your Score Says About Your Habits

Your credit score is not random. It's the mathematical reflection of patterns. It reveals how you handle due dates, how much debt you carry compared to your limits, how long you've managed credit, and how often you seek new credit. In other words, your score is a scoreboard—not of your identity—but of your habits over time.

The most important thing to understand is this: credit rewards consistency more than intensity. You don't have to make dramatic moves to improve your score—you need repeated good behavior. Paying on time consistently, lowering utilization, and avoiding frequent new inquiries often improves scores steadily. Small actions create momentum, and momentum creates a dopamine spike because you begin to see measurable change from discipline.

Your score also exposes financial stress patterns. High balances, late payments, and collections often reflect seasons of pressure, lack of structure, or avoidance—not lack of intelligence. That's why credit repair is rarely just paperwork. It's lifestyle alignment. When your cash flow is organized, your credit begins to heal naturally because you stop missing payments and stop leaning on debt for survival.

This is why FPS teaches you to treat credit like a mirror. If your score is low, it's not a reason for shame—it's a signal for adjustment. If your score is high, it's not a reason for pride—it's evidence that your habits are working. Scripture encourages this approach of honest evaluation: *"Let us examine our ways and test them…"* (Lamentations 3:40). Credit is one of the most objective tools for examining financial behavior without excuses.

Your Credit Reputation Audit

Credit is not judging you.
It is reporting on you.
Let's see exactly what it's saying.

Step 1: Pull Your Actual Reports

Go to AnnualCreditReport.com and download your reports from all three bureaus. Do not skip this step. Do not rely on memory. Look at documented evidence.

This is not about fear. It is about facts.

Step 2: Identify the Five Core Factors

Credit Reputation Audit Worksheet

Now evaluate yourself in each category.
Credit is Trust Documented. Build It Intentionally.

Name: ______________________________

Date:______________________________

Current Credit Snapshot

Current Credit Score: ______________________________

Score Goal (90 Days): ______________________________

Five Credit Factors Self-Assessment

Factor	Current Status	Needs Improvement?	Action Plan
Payment History			
Credit Utilization			
Length of Credit History			
New Credit Inquiries			
Credit Mix			

Primary Improvement Focus (Next 30–60 Days):

____

Commitment Statement:

My credit profile will reflect disciplined and reliable financial behavior.

Signature: ______________________________

Are you consistently on time? ☐ Yes ☐ No

Are your credit card balances above 30 percent of limits?
☐ Yes ☐ No

Do you have old accounts helping you—or did you close them? ☐ Yes ☐ No, closed

Have you applied for multiple accounts recently?
☐ Yes ☐ No

Is your credit diversified or concentrated? ☐ Yes ☐ No

This turns confusion into clarity.

Step 3: Score the Habits

For each category, give yourself a simple rating:

1. Strong
2. Needs Attention
3. Critical

Be honest. This is strategy, not self-criticism.

Step 4: Identify One Immediate Move

Choose one adjustment that will move your score within 30–60 days.

Examples:

Lower one card balance below 30 percent utilization.
Set up auto pay to eliminate late risk.
Stop applying for new credit.
Dispute one documented error.
You don't need ten changes. You need one decisive move.

Step 5: Write the Reputation Statement

Complete this sentence:

"My credit score reflects ________________________.

Over the next 90 days, it will reflect ______________."

This shifts identity from reactive to intentional.

Why This Exercise Works

It removes shame.
It removes mystery.
It creates control.
It creates a dopamine loop once the score begins responding.

You are no longer hoping your score improves.
You are engineering improvement.

Why Lenders See What You Ignore

Lenders don't see you the way you see you. They don't see your intentions. They don't see your future plans. They don't see that you "meant to pay" or that life got difficult. They see what is documented: payment history, debt levels, account age, and risk signals. That's why people feel shocked when they get denied—because they are judging themselves by their effort, while lenders judge by **evidence**.

This is also why many people unintentionally damage credit while thinking they're doing fine. They don't realize that carrying high credit card balances—even if payments are on time—can lower scores. They don't realize that closing old accounts can reduce average age of credit. They don't realize that multiple applications in a short period can signal desperation. The lender's view is not emotional—it's statistical.

Lenders also see patterns you stop noticing because they've become normal. That monthly "almost late" payment. That habit of maxing out then paying down. That cycle of applying for new credit to cover gaps. You may be used to it, but the algorithm sees it as risk. The good news is that once you understand what lenders see, you can stop accidentally sending red flags.

And this is where strategy becomes empowering. You can begin moving like someone who understands the system. You time your applications wisely. You lower utilization before major purchases. You clean up errors. You set auto pay and reminders. You stop letting oversight cost you money. Scripture speaks to living with wisdom and awareness: *"The prudent see danger and take refuge."* (Proverbs 22:3). Credit mastery is modern prudence—it's foresight that saves you cash and stress.

The Dopamine Moment: When Your Score Starts Responding

There's a specific moment in financial transformation that feels almost addictive—in the best way: when your actions start producing visible results. The first time you see your score rise after consistent on-time payments, or after paying down a card, something shifts. You stop feeling powerless and start feeling like a builder. That's the dopamine of progress, not impulse.

Credit improvement isn't magic—it's feedback. And feedback is fuel. Once you start receiving "proof" that your habits work, your motivation becomes internal. You no longer need hype. You have results. And results create momentum that spills into every part of the FPS system—debt elimination, savings, investing, and legacy-building.

Now that you understand credit as trust, what your score reveals, and how lenders evaluate risk, you're ready for the next vital step: **choosing your financial destination**. Because once you know where you are, the next question becomes powerful:

Where exactly are you going—and when will you arrive?

In the next part of FPS, we shift from assessment to vision. We stop reacting to money and start directing it.

You've built awareness.
Now you're about to build a future on purpose.

PART III – DECIDING ON YOUR DESTINATION

If you don't choose a destination, money will choose one for you.

If Part II helped you locate where you are, Part III is where you decide where you're going. This is the moment many people skip—and it's why they stay financially "busy" but never become financially free. When you don't choose a destination, your money defaults to whatever is loudest: bills, cravings, emergencies, social pressure, and convenience. That isn't a plan—that's financial autopilot.

A destination changes everything. It turns sacrifice into purpose. It turns discipline into direction. It turns "no" into a powerful "not yet." And once your destination is clear, your brain starts working with you instead of against you. Motivation becomes easier because you're no longer doing random financial tasks—you're moving toward a defined future.

Chapter 8: Defining Financial Freedom (Your Version)

Freedom vs. Luxury

Complete the following sentences:

Financial freedom means I can ________________

____.

I will know I am financially free when __________

____.

Freedom for my family looks like ______________

____.

Luxury I thought I wanted is _________________

____.

Peace for me feels like _____________________

____.

Is your current spending aligned with?

☐ freedom ☐ luxury

Most people think they want luxury when what they really crave is freedom. Luxury is about *having more*. Freedom is about *needing less to feel secure and in control.* Luxury is often external—status, brands, upgrades. Freedom is internal—peace, options, stability, and the ability to make decisions without panic. If you chase luxury without defining freedom, you can end up with expensive possessions and still feel trapped.

Financial freedom means your life is no longer dictated by financial stress. It means bills don't scare you, emergencies don't break you, and opportunities don't feel impossible. Freedom looks like having savings, having a plan, and having margin. It's being able to say "yes" to what matters and "no" to what drains you—without guilt and without fear. It's waking up without that tight feeling in your chest when you think about money.

Luxury isn't wrong—but luxury without structure becomes a trap.

List 5 recent purchases, then for each purchase, choose the best category for each:

Did this increase:

1. Freedom
2. Pressure
3. Temporary pleasure
4. Long-term stability

Purchase	Amount	Category

How much was spent on these 5 purchases: $______________

Now ask yourself:

If I redirected this money for 12 months, what would change?

____

____

____

____

____

____

Many people finance luxury and call it success, while quietly carrying anxiety, debt, and pressure. Real freedom is when you can afford what you enjoy *without borrowing peace to pay for it.* The goal isn't to eliminate enjoyment; the goal is to eliminate dependence. When you define freedom properly, luxury becomes optional—something you choose wisely—not something you chase emotionally.

Scripture captures this difference with surprising clarity: *"Godliness with contentment is great gain."* (1 Timothy 6:6). Contentment doesn't mean small dreams—it means your joy isn't held hostage by your purchases. It means you can build without desperation and enjoy without bondage. When freedom becomes the goal, your money finally has direction—and direction creates momentum.

Lifestyle Design

Lifestyle design is choosing your life on purpose instead of living by default. Most people build their finances around emergencies and obligations, then wonder why they never feel ahead. Lifestyle design flips the script. It asks: What kind of life do you want to live? What kind of mornings do you want? What type of stress level do you want? What do you want your weekends to feel like? What do you want your family to experience because you were disciplined?

Here's the breakthrough: lifestyle design is not fantasy—it's planning with clarity. It means you decide what matters most—family time, travel, flexibility, entrepreneurship, ministry, legacy—and you align your spending to support it. Your budget stops being a list of restrictions and becomes a blueprint for your life. That shift alone makes people excited to manage money, because money stops feeling like punishment and starts feeling like possibility.

To eliminate uncertainty, think of lifestyle design in categories:

- Time
- Location
- Work
- Relationships
- Health
- Peace

Do you want more time freedom or more income right now?

☐ Time freedom ☐ Income

Do you want to travel annually or build a larger emergency fund first?

☐ Time freedom ☐ Income

Do you want to own a home, start a business, or reduce work hours?

☐ Own a home ☐ Start a business ☐ Reduce work hours

Your answers determine your destination. The point is not to copy someone else's goals. The point is to define yours with honesty and intention.

Scripture supports this idea of intentional building: *"Write the vision and make it plain…"* (Habakkuk 2:2). "Plain" means clear enough to follow. Lifestyle design is writing your financial vision so clearly that your daily decisions can obey it. And once your lifestyle is defined, every dollar you spend starts asking a question: Does this help build the life I said I want?

Peace, Not Pressure

Before I talk about this section, I need you to answer a few questions.

On a scale of 1-10:

How much peace do I feel about my finances right now?

1	2	3	4	5	6	7	8	9	10

What is the single biggest source of financial pressure in your life? ________________________.

What one move would reduce that pressure within 30 days?

____.

Many people pursue money hoping it will finally bring peace, but they chase it in a way that produces pressure. They overwork, overspend, over borrow, and overextend—then wonder why they feel anxious even when they earn more. That's because peace is not produced by income alone. Peace is produced by alignment, stability, margin, and self-trust. Peace happens when your money habits support your life instead of strangling it.

Real financial freedom is the ability to breathe. It's having enough structure that you're not afraid of the unknown. It's knowing your bills are covered, your savings is growing, your debt is shrinking, and your future is being funded. Peace is not flashy, but it is priceless. And once you taste peace—even a small amount—you stop craving financial chaos. You begin craving order. Progress becomes satisfying.

Pressure-driven finances usually come from trying to look successful instead of becoming stable. Pressure makes people rush. It makes them take shortcuts. It makes them borrow to impress, spend to soothe, and avoid planning because planning feels like admitting reality. Peace does the opposite. Peace allows you to face the numbers calmly, follow the plan consistently, and make decisions that your future self will thank you for.

Scripture anchors this beautifully without overload: *"For God is not the author of confusion, but of peace."* (1 Corinthians 14:33). Confusion is expensive. Peace is profitable. The destination of FPS is not merely "more money." The destination is a life where money no longer controls your emotions, your choices, or your confidence.

And here's the dopamine shift: when peace becomes the goal, your progress becomes exciting. Every debt payment feels like pressure leaving your body. Every deposit into savings feels like oxygen entering your future. Every wise decision becomes proof that you're changing your life in real time.

Now that you've defined financial freedom—your version—it's time to go from vision to clarity. In the next chapter, we will build your ideal future with precision: what you want, why you want it, and how to turn it into measurable goals that keep you focused when temptation shows up.

You've chosen a destination.
Now your mind will stop wandering—and your money will start moving.

Chapter 9: Vision Casting Your Financial Future

Because when the future becomes clear, discipline becomes easier—and progress becomes inevitable.

A vision is not wishful thinking. A vision is a decision about who you're becoming and what your money will support. Without vision, your finances will be governed by whatever is urgent today. But when you can see your future clearly, something powerful happens: your mind stops negotiating with impulses, and your habits start aligning with purpose.

This chapter is where you move from "I want to do better" to "I know exactly what I'm building." Vision creates emotional energy. It spikes motivation in a healthy way because you're no longer sacrificing for vague outcomes—you're investing in a future you can actually picture. And the clearer the picture, the more consistent you become.

One-Year, Five-Year, Generational Vision

Your one-year vision is your **stabilization plan**. It answers the question: what would financial improvement look like in the next 12 months if you took this seriously? For many people, the one-year vision includes debt reduction, a starter emergency fund, fewer late payments, fewer money arguments, and more breathing room. It's not about perfection—it's about traction. In one year, you should be able to point to real proof that your life is different.

Exercise: The One-Year Stabilization Plan

Close your eyes for 60 seconds and imagine your financial life one year from now.

Now write it:

One year from today, my financial life looks like this:

My debt balance is: $__________________

My savings balance is: $__________________

My stress level is: ______________________

My relationship with money feels: __________________

My monthly surplus is: $__________________

Here's what makes the one-year vision dopamine-rich: it's close enough to feel real. You can practically touch it. You can measure it month by month. It's the kind of vision that makes you wake up with purpose because you know what you're aiming at. This is where you decide your next 12 months will no longer be a repeat of the last 12. The one-year vision is where momentum begins—and momentum is one of the most empowering feelings a person can experience.

Your five-year vision is your **expansion plan**. It answers: what should be true in five years if I stay consistent? In five years, debt should be greatly reduced or eliminated, credit should be strong, savings should be substantial, and retirement contributions should be flowing regularly. Five years is long enough for compounding to begin working in your favor—financially, emotionally, and relationally. This is also where asset-building becomes realistic: home ownership, investment accounts, business launch, or income expansion.

Five-Year Expansion Blueprint

In the worksheet below write in your current value of each category and then write in what you want them to be in five years.

Category	Current Reality	Five-Year Target
Net Worth	$	$
Debt Level	$	$
Savings	$	$
Investments	$	$
Home Equity	$	$
Business/Side Income	$	$
Retirement Contributions	$	$

If I stay consistent for five years, what becomes inevitable?

____

____

____

____

This builds belief through compounding logic.

Then comes the generational vision—your **legacy plan**. This is where you stop thinking like a consumer and start thinking like an architect. Generational vision asks: what should my children, grandchildren, or community experience because I decided to master money instead of being mastered by it? Legacy isn't just "leaving money." It's leaving systems: financial literacy, estate planning, insurance protection, property, businesses, and values. It's making sure your family inherits stability instead of stress.

Exercise: Generational Legacy Map

What systems will exist because you got disciplined?

- ☐College funds
- ☐Estate plan
- ☐Life insurance
- ☐Property
- ☐Family financial meetings
- ☐Business ownership
- ☐Investment accounts

What cycle ends with you? ______________________________

Scripture frames this kind of thinking as wisdom, not arrogance: *"A good man leaves an inheritance to his children's children…"* (Proverbs 13:22). Generational vision is not about showing off—it's about breaking cycles. It's about making sure the next generation starts ahead instead of starting over. And once you develop a generational vision, your daily discipline stops feeling small—because it becomes connected to something bigger than you.

Income Goals, Savings Goals, Legacy Goals

Vision becomes powerful when it becomes specific. That's why you need three categories of goals that work together: **income goals, savings goals, and legacy goals**. Income goals answer: how much money needs to come in to support the life I'm designing? Savings goals answer: how much must I keep to create stability and opportunity? Legacy goals answer: what am I building that will outlive my labor?

Income goals should not be based only on desire—they should be based on requirements. Start with your monthly cost of living, add your debt payoff target, add your savings targets, add your giving goals, and then calculate the income required to support that plan without stress. This is where many people get clarity: they realize that the goal isn't "more money," it's "enough money structured correctly." When income goals are rooted in reality, they become achievable rather than fantasy.

Savings goals are your protection goals. They are the difference between an inconvenience and a crisis. A basic emergency fund protects you from falling back into debt when life happens. A sinking fund helps you prepare for predictable expenses like car repairs, holidays, school expenses, or travel. A retirement fund protects your future self from becoming financially dependent on others. Savings goals create peace because they remove fear of the unknown.

Legacy goals bring purpose to the plan. This is where you decide to build something lasting: paying off a home, purchasing investment property, funding your children's education, creating life insurance protection, writing a will or trust, starting a business, or creating a family financial playbook. Legacy goals turn financial discipline into a mission. They give your money spiritual and emotional meaning beyond consumption.

Scripture supports this pattern of purposeful preparation: *"The wise store up choice food and olive oil, but fools gulp theirs down."* (Proverbs 21:20). Storing up isn't hoarding—it's planning. It's wisdom in motion. And when you pair clear income goals with intentional savings goals and legacy-focused building, your future stops being uncertain. It becomes engineered.

Making Vision Practical Without Feeling Overwhelmed

To eliminate uncertainty, here's the simplest way to build your vision without getting stuck: write your one-year vision in outcomes, your five-year vision in assets, and your generational vision in systems. Outcomes are things like "debt reduced by X" or "credit score increased to Y." Assets are things like "savings at X" or "retirement account funded consistently." Systems are things like "estate plan completed," "insurance coverage in place," "family financial education established."

When you do this, vision becomes a map—not a dream. You can look at it, measure it, and track it. And once you can track it, you can win. Winning is addictive. Progress becomes exciting. And your brain begins to crave the feeling of alignment more than the feeling of impulse.

Exercise: The Reverse Engineering Plan

If five years is the destination, what must be true in three years? ____.

If three years is the checkpoint, what must be true in one year? ____.

If one year is the checkpoint, what must be true in 90 days? ____.

Exercise: The Vision Lock Statement

Fill in the blank and write it out:

"I am building ______________________________.
I will not trade long-term vision for short-term comfort.
My discipline today protects my legacy tomorrow."

Now the future is no longer abstract. It's scheduled. Now that your future is clear, it's time to turn vision into measurable targets you can execute. In the next chapter, we'll take what you've defined and convert it into **SMART financial goals**—specific, measurable, achievable, relevant, and time-bound—so you always know exactly what to do next.

You've seen the future.
Now you're going to build it—one measurable step at a time.

Chapter 10: Setting SMART Financial Goals

Vision becomes real when it becomes measurable—and measurable becomes achievable.

A dream is inspiring, but a goal is executable. Dreams live in your imagination; goals live on your calendar. That's why this chapter matters so much. You've already located your financial starting point and cast a vision for your future. Now we take the next powerful step: converting your vision into **SMART goals**—Specific, Measurable, Achievable, Relevant, and Time-bound.

SMART goals spike momentum because they remove uncertainty. They give your brain a target, a timeline, and a clear win condition. Instead of saying, "I want to get out of debt," you'll say, "I will pay off $8,400 in 10 months by paying $840 per month plus $200 extra from redirected leaks." That level of clarity turns hope into certainty—and certainty is fuel.

Exercise: The SMART Conversion Lab

Rewrite three these vague goals into SMART goals.

Vague Goal: "I want to save more."

SMART Version: ________________________________

Vague Goal: "I want to improve my credit."

SMART Version: ________________________________

Vague Goal: "I want to get out of debt."

SMART Version: ________________________________

What is the exact date these goal will be completed?

Debt Payoff Timelines

Debt payoff becomes realistic when you stop treating debt like a cloud and start treating it like a list. A timeline begins with one simple equation: **total debt ÷ monthly payoff amount = estimated months to freedom**. That's it. Not magic. Not vibes. Just math and consistency. The moment you calculate your timeline, something powerful happens emotionally: the debt stops feeling endless.

Exercise: Debt Freedom Timeline Builder

1. Write Total Debt: $__________
2. Write Monthly Payoff Amount: $__________
3. Divide to determine Estimated Months to Freedom:

   It will take me ________ months to achieve Freedom

Create two timelines:

Minimum Plan: ______ months
Stretch Plan: ______ months

What will your life feel like when this date arrives? _________

____

Now debt is no longer abstract. It has a finish line.

To make your timeline SMART, you must be specific about the type of debt and the order you'll attack it. You can choose a snowball approach (smallest balance first for quick wins), an avalanche approach (highest interest first for maximum savings), or a hybrid approach (quick wins plus interest strategy). The key is not which method is "best"—the key is which method you'll actually follow without quitting. Consistency beats perfection every time.

Your debt payoff timeline also needs built-in flexibility. Life will happen. A tire will blow. A medical bill may show up. A month may be tighter than expected. SMART planning accounts for reality. This is where you create a "minimum required payment plan" and a "stretch payoff plan." Minimum keeps you moving no matter what. Stretch accelerates progress when extra money appears. That way, setbacks don't destroy the plan—they just slow the speed temporarily.

Here's where dopamine gets involved: debt payoff becomes addictive when you see movement. Paying off one account creates momentum. Momentum creates belief. Belief creates discipline. Your brain begins to crave the feeling of progress more than the feeling of purchases. And scripture supports the power of steady progress: *"Do not despise these small beginnings…"* (Zechariah 4:10). Small beginnings lead to big endings when the timeline is clear and the steps are consistent.

Credit Score Targets

A credit score goal becomes SMART when it is tied to a purpose, not vanity. Don't just say, "I want a 750." Ask: what will that score allow me to do? Lower interest rates? Qualify for a mortgage? Reduce insurance premiums? Fund a business? When your credit target is connected to a life outcome, discipline becomes easier because the goal has meaning.

To set credit score targets correctly, you must start with your current score and identify the categories most likely holding you back: payment history, utilization, derogatory marks, average age, and inquiries. Even if you don't memorize every category, you can set a SMART target like: "Increase my score by 40 points in 90 days by paying all payments on time and reducing utilization below 30%." That's specific and measurable.

Credit goals should be time-bound in stages. Instead of "get to 750 someday," set milestone targets: 30 days, 90 days, 6 months, 12 months. Credit improvement is often gradual—but the milestones make it exciting. You start collecting wins. You start seeing the system respond. And the moment the score rises, your confidence rises with it.

Exercise: The Credit Score Target Map

Tie your score to outcome.

What is your Current Score: ________

What is your 90-Day Target: ________

What is your 12-Month Target: ________

This score will allow you to: ____________________________

Create a 30-day action checklist:

☐ Reduce utilization
☐ Set auto pay

☐ Avoid new inquiries
☐ Dispute inaccuracies

This shifts you from wishing to engineering.

Scripture emphasizes the power of a trustworthy reputation: *"A good name is more desirable than great riches."* (Proverbs 22:1). In today's world, credit is a modern "good name" financially. It's not your identity—it's your reliability score. And as you improve it, you're not just raising a number—you're increasing access, lowering costs, and expanding your options.

Emergency, Opportunity, and Retirement Goals

Most people treat savings like a leftover category—whatever remains after spending. SMART savers reverse that mindset. They pay themselves intentionally because they understand this: **savings is not what you do after life happens; savings is what prepares you before life happens.** This section will help you set three types of savings goals that cover your present and protect your future.

Emergency goals are the foundation. An emergency fund turns disasters into inconveniences. Instead of swiping a credit card when life happens, you handle it with cash and stay on your debt-free path. A SMART emergency goal might be: "Save $1,000 in 8 weeks by saving $125 per week from redirected leaks and a fixed savings transfer." Once you hit $1,000, you can build toward 1–3 months of expenses, then 3–6 months. The point is to build layers of protection.

Opportunity goals are what separate surviving from thriving. Opportunity funds are for planned growth and enjoyment: vacations, education, a business launch, a vehicle upgrade, moving costs, a home down payment, or a major life event.

These funds prevent you from borrowing for what you could prepare for. A SMART opportunity goal might be: "Save $2,400 for a vacation by saving $200 per month for 12 months." This keeps joy in your life without stealing from your future.

Retirement goals are where legacy thinking becomes real. Retirement isn't old age—it's financial independence. It's the ability to live without depending on a job, a child, or a crisis donation. A SMART retirement goal might be: "Contribute $150 per month to my retirement account starting this month, increasing by $25 every 90 days." Retirement goals work best when they are automated, consistent, and steadily increased over time.

Scripture supports preparation with wisdom and balance: *"The wise store up choice food and olive oil…"* (Proverbs 21:20). That verse isn't about fear—it's about foresight. Saving isn't hoarding; it's stewardship. And when you build emergency, opportunity, and retirement goals simultaneously—at the right pace—you create a life that feels stable now and secure later.

Now that you have SMART goals for debt, credit, and savings, the next step is making sure your money aligns with what matters most—your values. Because goals without values feel heavy, and money without values gets wasted.

In the next chapter, we'll align your financial goals with your priorities so every dollar supports your purpose, not just your bills.

You've set the targets.
Now you're going to give every dollar meaning.

Chapter 11: Aligning Money with Values

When your money matches what matters, stress decreases and progress accelerates.

One of the greatest reasons people feel financial pressure—even when they make decent money—is not because they lack income. It's because their spending is not aligned with their values. When money flows in a direction that doesn't match what you truly care about, it creates internal conflict. You can't spend against your values and still feel peace. Your bank account may survive it, but your spirit won't enjoy it.

This chapter is where financial freedom becomes deeper than debt payoff. This is where money stops being just math and becomes meaning. When your goals and values are aligned, discipline becomes easier because you're no longer forcing yourself to "be good with money." You're simply living in agreement with what you believe matters most.

Exercise: The Values Discovery Audit

My top five values are:

1. ______________________________

2. ______________________________

3. ______________________________

4. ______________________________

5. ______________________________________

Now:

The five categories where I spend the most money are:

1. ______________________________________
2. ______________________________________
3. ______________________________________
4. ______________________________________
5. ______________________________________

Do these two lists match? ☐ Yes ☐ No

Where is the disconnect? ☐ Yes ☐ No

What category reveals the greatest misalignment?

____

This creates immediate conviction without shame.

Giving, Stewardship, and Purpose

Giving is not just a religious concept—it's a values concept. Even people who aren't faith-driven still believe in supporting something bigger than themselves: family, community, causes, and legacy. Giving becomes powerful when it is intentional instead of emotional. Emotional giving happens from guilt, pressure, or urgency. Intentional giving happens from purpose, planning, and peace. FPS teaches that giving should never be random; it should be rooted in your vision.

Stewardship is the mindset that everything you have is managed, not merely owned. Stewardship says, "I'm responsible for how I handle what comes into my hands." This shifts money from being a source of anxiety into being a tool of assignment. Stewardship doesn't make you perfect—it makes you purposeful. It helps you stop asking, "How can I spend this?" and start asking, "How can I maximize this?"

Purpose is what makes discipline feel worth it. When money is connected to purpose, saving becomes exciting, debt payoff becomes meaningful, and budgeting stops feeling like punishment. Purpose gives your financial decisions direction.

2. Exercise: Giving, Stewardship, and Purpose Reflection

Ask yourself:

What do I believe my money is meant to do beyond paying bills?

Who or what do I feel called to support consistently?

What kind of impact do I want my money to make in my family, community, or future?

Then ask:

Am I currently spending like a consumer, or managing like a steward?

Instead of chasing temporary pleasure, you begin funding lasting outcomes: stability for your household, education for your children, freedom for your future, and impact for your community.

Scripture supports this without needing to overwhelm you: *"Moreover, it is required in stewards that one be found faithful."* (1 Corinthians 4:2). Faithfulness is not about being flawless—it's about being consistent and intentional. When you operate as a steward, you don't panic when money is tight; you prioritize. You don't get reckless when money is abundant; you plan. Stewardship keeps you stable in every season.

Here's the dopamine shift: when you align giving with purpose and stewardship, you start feeling proud of your money decisions again. You stop feeling like money is disappearing.

You start feeling like money is **building**. And nothing fuels progress like the feeling that your life is finally moving in the right direction.

Why Misaligned Money Always Causes Stress

Misalignment is expensive—emotionally, relationally, and financially. Misalignment happens when your money says one thing, but your values say another. You say family matters, but your spending leaves no margin for experiences. You say peace matters, but you keep financing stress through debt. You say legacy matters, but you never invest or save. The stress doesn't come from money itself—it comes from the **tension** between what you believe and what you're doing.

Complete the following:

I say I value: ____________________

But my spending shows: ____________________

I say I want peace, but I keep funding: ____________________

I say I want legacy, but I keep delaying: ____________________

One spending habit that keeps violating my values is:

____

This reveals the real issue: not lack of money, but divided priorities.

This is why some people feel guilty even when they buy something small. The purchase isn't always wrong—it's just out of alignment. Misaligned spending creates a sense of internal betrayal: "Why did I do that again?" Over time, that repeated betrayal damages self-trust. And when self-trust is weak, discipline feels harder because you don't believe your own promises anymore.

One promise I keep making but not keeping is:

____

The reason I keep breaking this promise is:

____

One small financial promise I can keep this week is:

____

Make the following declaration:

I rebuild self-trust by keeping small promises consistently.

This helps your turn shame into momentum.

Misalignment also creates conflict in relationships. Couples argue when one person's values are being funded and the other persons are being ignored. Families struggle when money is consumed by lifestyle instead of stability. Individuals feel lonely with money decisions because they're funding image instead of purpose. When money is misaligned, it doesn't just drain accounts—it drains emotional energy.

What does my household say matters most?

What does our spending actually prioritize?

Where does money create the most tension in our relationships?

What one financial change would bring more unity into our home?

This makes the chapter relational, not just personal.

Scripture addresses this principle in a way that applies perfectly to finance: *"No one can serve two masters…"* (Matthew 6:24). Misaligned money is what it looks like to serve competing priorities—comfort vs. freedom, image vs. stability, impulse vs. purpose. The stress is the signal that your life is being pulled in opposite directions. Alignment brings relief because it creates one clear direction.

The solution is not to become extreme. The solution is to become intentional. You decide what matters most and assign money accordingly—first. Then you build enjoyment around that structure. When values lead and spending follows, stress decreases dramatically. You stop feeling like you're constantly catching up, constantly guilty, constantly pressured. You gain the priceless feeling of being in control.

Making Values Practical: The "Values Budget"

To remove uncertainty, here's the simplest way to apply this chapter: create a "Values Budget." List your top values—faith, family, health, education, peace, legacy, generosity, travel, entrepreneurship—whatever is truly yours.

My Top Value: ____________________
How I will fund it monthly: ____________________
Amount: $__________

My Top Value: ____________________
How I will fund it monthly: ____________________
Amount: $__________

My Top Value: ____________________
How I will fund it monthly: ____________________
Amount: $__________

Then look at your spending and ask,

Does my money reflect this?

What spending category must decrease to make room for what matters most?

You don't need perfection. You need direction.

A values budget doesn't eliminate fun—it protects it. Because when the important things are funded first, enjoyment stops producing guilt. When you know your savings is growing and your debt is shrinking, you can enjoy the occasional treat without feeling like you're harming your future. Alignment makes joy clean. Misalignment makes joy expensive.

Does this purchase reflect my values? ☐ Yes ☐ No
Does this move me toward peace or pressure?
☐ Peace ☐ Pressure
Does this my future or steal from it? ☐ Support ☐ Steal
Will I feel aligned after buying this? ☐ Yes ☐ No

Now that your values and money are aligned, it's time to decide:

This week, I will make one financial decision that clearly reflects what matters most to me.

That decision is: ______________________________

This week, I will reduce or eliminate one expense that conflicts with my values.

That expense is: ______________________________

You've aligned your heart.
Now you're going to align your actions—and start moving like someone who knows exactly where they're going.

PART IV – DEVELOPING YOUR ROUTE

Your route determines your speed, safety, and sustainability.

Now that you've located your starting point and chosen your destination, it's time to do what a GPS does best: **build the route**. A destination without a route is still a dream. A route turns vision into steps. And the right route doesn't just get you there—it gets you there with less stress, fewer detours, and a much higher chance of staying free once you arrive.

Here's the key: there is no single "best" strategy for everyone. There is only the best strategy for **you**—your personality, your cash flow, your income stability, your discipline level, and your season of life. This chapter is designed to remove uncertainty by giving you clear options, clear tradeoffs, and clear reasons to choose one route over another.

Chapter 12: Choosing the Right Financial Strategy

Snowball vs. Avalanche Debt Methods

Debt payoff strategies fail when people choose methods that look smart on paper but don't match how humans actually behave. That's why FPS treats debt payoff like navigation: your goal isn't just math—it's **momentum**. The two most proven routes are the **Snowball Method** and the **Avalanche Method**, and both work when applied consistently.

Exercise: Debt Strategy Fit Assessment

When I make financial progress, what motivates me most?

- ☐ Quick wins
- ☐ Long-term savings
- ☐ A mix of both

When I feel discouraged, what helps me continue?

- ☐ Visible progress
- ☐ Mathematical proof
- ☐ External accountability

Do I need momentum fast, or can I stay committed without immediate wins? ____

Based on my behavior, not just my opinion, which method fits me best?

☐ Snowball
☐ Avalanche
☐ Hybrid

The **Snowball Method** focuses on paying off the smallest debt first (while paying minimums on the rest). Once the smallest debt is eliminated, you roll that payment into the next smallest debt, and so on—like a snowball gaining size and speed. Snowball is powerful because it creates quick wins. Those early wins' spike dopamine and build belief. You start thinking, "I can actually do this." That belief is not emotional fluff—it becomes fuel for consistency.

The **Avalanche Method** focuses on paying off the debt with the highest interest rate first (while paying minimums on the rest). This method is mathematically efficient because it reduces the total interest you pay over time, which can save hundreds or even thousands of dollars. Avalanche is ideal for people who are highly disciplined and motivated by long-term savings rather than quick wins.

Snowball vs. Avalanche Comparison Sheet

	Snowball	**Avalanche**
First Debt		
Balance	$	$
Estimated payoff time		
Estimated interest saving		

Which plan would I actually follow for the next 90 days without quitting? ☐ Snowball ☐ Avalanche

So which one should you choose? Choose the method you will **stick with**. If you need motivation and confidence, snowball often wins because it builds momentum fast. If you are steady, strategic, and want maximum savings, avalanche may fit you better. My opinion: many people do best with a **hybrid approach**—get one or two quick wins with snowball to build momentum, then switch to avalanche to attack high-interest predators.

My Chosen Debt Route Statement

My chosen debt strategy is: ______________________________

I chose this strategy because: ____________________________

____

The first debt I will target is: ___________________________

My monthly focused payment amount will be: $_____________

My reason for staying consistent is: _______________________

Scripture supports the principle behind both methods: progress is built step by step. *"Do not despise these small beginnings…"* (Zechariah 4:10). Whether you start with the smallest balance or the highest interest, your route works when you stay faithful to consistent, measurable progress.

Income Increase vs. Expense Reduction

To build speed in your financial journey, you have two main levers: **increase income** or **reduce expenses**. Most people try to do only one, which slows progress and increases frustration. The truth is, the fastest route usually combines both—because income creates power, and expense reduction creates margin.

Expense reduction is the fastest lever to pull because you can do it immediately. You can cancel subscriptions today. You can reduce convenience spending today. You can renegotiate bills today. You can change grocery habits today. Expense reduction is often where "hidden money" is found.

Expense Reduction Audit

List 5 expenses you can reduce this week:

1. ______________________________
2. ______________________________
3. ______________________________
4. ______________________________
5. ______________________________

Potential monthly savings from these changes: $__________

Now:

What one expense reduction would create the fastest breathing room?

____

This is why people get a rush of hope when they finally track spending—because they discover they had more control than they realized.

But expense reduction alone has limits. You can only cut so far before you start feeling deprived or restricted. That's why **income increase** becomes the long-term accelerator. Income increase can come from overtime, side work, selling unused items, launching a small business, learning a high-income skill, or leveraging the Debt Conqueror opportunity structure if you're aligned with it. Income increase gives you the ability to pay off debt faster, build savings sooner, and invest earlier.

Income Increase Brainstorm

Income I can increase immediately: ______________________

Items I can sell in the next 14 days: ______________________

Skills I can monetize: ___________________________________

Side income idea I can test this month: __________________

Long-term income strategy I should build: ________________

Then ask:

Which one can produce income the fastest? _______________

Which one has the highest long-term potential? ___________

Here's the strategy that eliminates uncertainty: reduce expenses to create immediate breathing room, then increase income to create long-term acceleration. Expense reduction stabilizes the boat; income increase adds the engine.

This month, I will reduce expenses by: $________

This month, I will increase income by: $________

Total additional money I can redirect toward my goals: $________

That total will go toward:

☐ Debt
☐ Savings
☐ Emergency Fund
☐ Mixed Allocation

When you do both, your debt payoff timeline can shrink dramatically—not by luck, but by design.

Scripture points to this dual approach—wisdom and work. *"The plans of the diligent lead surely to abundance…"* (Proverbs 21:5). Plans include expense strategy. Diligence includes income strategy. Together, they create momentum that feels exciting because your efforts produce visible results.

Automation vs. Manual Control

One of the biggest reasons people fail financially isn't lack of knowledge—it's inconsistency caused by human nature. We forget. We get busy. We get emotional. We get distracted. That's why a powerful route includes a decision: will you rely on **manual control**, or will you build **automation** to protect your progress?

Automation vs. Manual Control Profile

I usually forget financial tasks when I am:

☐ Debt
☐ Savings
☐ Emergency Fund
☐ Mixed Allocation

I prefer managing money:

☐ Hands-on
☐ Semi-automated
☐ Fully automated

Do I need more awareness first, or more automation first?
☐ Awareness ☐ Automation

Manual control means you consciously manage every step: paying bills manually, moving money manually, tracking spending manually, and making decisions actively. Manual control can work well for people who love being hands-on and enjoy the feeling of direct oversight. It can also be beneficial early on because it forces awareness and builds discipline.

But manual control has a weakness: it depends on your mood and memory. If you're stressed, busy, or discouraged, manual systems break down. That's why **automation** is a financial cheat code. Automation pays bills on time, transfers money to savings, and moves funds toward debt consistently—without waiting for motivation. Automation turns your plan into a system that runs even when life is chaotic.

A balanced approach usually wins: manually track and review weekly, but automate the essential movements—minimum payments, savings transfers, and targeted debt payments.

Weekly spending review	Manual	Automatic
Budget adjustments		
Goal tracking		
Minimum debt payments		
Savings transfers		
Bill payments		
Targeted extra payment		
Other:		

The first automation I will set up is: ___________________

The first manual review day I will commit to is: / /

That way, your foundation stays consistent, and your weekly check-ins become strategic adjustments, not emergency interventions. You don't have to be perfect—your system keeps you stable.

Scripture supports the concept of building systems that keep you steady: *"Let all things be done decently and in order."* (1 Corinthians 14:40). Financial order isn't rigid—it's protective. Automation is one of the most practical forms of order because it removes the opportunity for your emotions to interrupt your destiny.

Now that you've chosen your strategy—Decide on these:

Strategy Summary

My debt method is: ___________________

My expense reduction target is: $________

My income increase target is: $________

My key automation is: ___________________

My weekly financial review day is: ___________________

This week, the first action I will take is: ___________________

Since you have decided how you'll attack debt, increase speed, and build consistency—it's time to turn your strategy into a step-by-step roadmap you can actually follow without feeling overwhelmed.

In the next chapter, we're going to break your long-term goals into small, clear actions that create daily and weekly wins. This is where the route becomes real.

You've chosen the route.
Now you're going to start moving—one confident step at a time.

Chapter 13: Breaking Big Goals into Action Steps

Big goals don't require big stress—only small steps done consistently.

One of the fastest ways people quit a financial plan is not because the plan is bad, but because the plan feels too big. Big goals create big emotions. And when emotions rise, clarity drops. That's why this chapter exists: to turn your financial destination into **daily movement** that feels doable, measurable, and rewarding.

The secret is simple: you don't conquer debt, build savings, and raise credit "all at once." You do it through a series of small, repeatable actions that compound over time. When your actions are organized into monthly, weekly, and daily rhythms, money stops feeling chaotic and starts feeling like a system you can actually run. That's when progress becomes exciting—because you can see yourself winning again and again.

Goal Breakdown Map

My big financial goal is: ____________________

To reach that goal, I must accomplish these 3 smaller goals:

1. ____________________
2. ____________________
3. ____________________

This month, my priority is: ____________________
This week, my focus is: ____________________
Today, my next action is: ____________________

You should be in execution mode now!

Monthly, Weekly, Daily Money Actions

A strong financial route has three levels: monthly decisions, weekly adjustments, and daily discipline. Think of it like a GPS route: the **monthly plan** is your overall journey map, the **weekly check-in** is your reroute feature, and the **daily actions** are the turns you take to stay on course. When all three are working together, you no longer rely on motivation—you rely on structure.

Monthly, Weekly, Daily Money Rhythm Builder

Monthly Money Actions:

____

____

____

Weekly Money Actions:

____

____

____

Daily Money Actions:

____

____

____

Which of these levels am I strongest in?

☐ Monthly
☐ Weekly
☐ Daily

Which level is currently breaking down my progress?

☐ Monthly
☐ Weekly
☐ Daily

Your **monthly money actions** set your financial direction. This includes creating your monthly spending plan, assigning dollar amounts to categories, scheduling your debt payments, setting your savings transfers, and reviewing upcoming expenses. A monthly plan isn't about perfection; it's about preparation. It is the moment you take control before the month starts taking control of you.

My Monthly Financial Focus Plan

This month, I am primarily focusing on:

☐ Debt reduction
☐ Savings
☐ Current bills
☐ Credit improvement
☐ Mixed priority

My top 3 money priorities this month are:

1. ______________________________

2. ______________________________

3. ____________________

Extra money this month will go toward: ________________

Upcoming expenses I must prepare for: ________________

This makes the month intentional before the month begins. It's also where you make strategic decisions like, "This month, we're focusing on extra payments," or "This month, we're rebuilding savings after an emergency."

Your **weekly money actions** keep you from drifting. This is where most people win or lose, because money doesn't leak monthly—it leaks daily. Weekly actions include reviewing your bank account, checking category spending, confirming bills are paid, and adjusting for real-life changes. Weekly check-ins are not punishment; they are protection. They are how you catch problems while they're small, so they never become crises. Weekly check-ins also create a confidence boost because you stop feeling surprised by money.

Weekly Money Check-In Template

Each week I will review:

Bank balance: ________________

Bills due this week: ________________

Category overspending: ________________

Progress toward debt/savings goal: ________________

Adjustment needed this week: ________________

My weekly money review day will be: ____________________

This turns "check-ins" into an actual system.

Your **daily money actions** are the smallest, simplest behaviors that keep the whole system stable. These include pausing before purchases, checking balances, tracking spending (even briefly), using a list when shopping, avoiding impulsive online browsing, and staying aware of your financial goals. Daily actions build identity. They teach your brain, "I'm the kind of person who manages money on purpose."

Daily Discipline Checklist

Today I:

- ☐ Paused before unnecessary spending
- ☐ Checked my account or spending
- ☐ Remembered my financial goal
- ☐ Avoided an impulse purchase
- ☐ Followed my spending plan

Which daily habit would strengthen your financial identity the most?

____

This helps you build identity through repetition. And that identity shift is one of the most powerful forces in financial transformation.

Scripture supports the value of small consistent steps: *"Whoever is faithful in little will be faithful also in much."* (Luke 16:10). Daily "little" decisions become monthly outcomes. Monthly outcomes become life results. When you learn to operate on all three levels—monthly, weekly, daily—you stop being reactive and start becoming financially intentional.

Removing Overwhelm

Overwhelm is not a money problem—it's a clarity problem. People feel overwhelmed because they're holding too many decisions in their head at once. Bills, debts, credit, savings, goals—it all feels like a foggy pile of pressure. The solution isn't trying harder. The solution is breaking the pressure into clear actions you can execute one step at a time.

The first way to eliminate overwhelm is to reduce your focus to a **few priority targets**. Instead of trying to fix everything at once, you identify the "Big 3" for the next 30 days: for example, "Stay current on bills, pay extra on one debt, and build a starter emergency fund."

The Big 3 Focus Filter

My Big 3 Financial Priorities for the Next 30 Days:

1. ____
2. ____
3. ____

If I complete these three things, my financial life will improve because:

____

What must I ignore or postpone in order to protect these priorities?

This reduces mental clutter and drives execution. When your brain has a short list, it calms down. When it calms down, it can execute. This is how you move from anxiety to action.

The second way to remove overwhelm is to create **defaults**—automatic choices that reduce decision fatigue. Auto pay for minimum payments. Automatic savings transfers. A set day each week for a 15-minute money check-in. A rule like "24-hour pause before non-essential purchases." Defaults keep you moving even when you're tired.

Default Decision Builder

One bill I will automate: ______________________________

One savings transfer I will automate: ____________________

My weekly check-in day and time: ______________________

My 24-hour purchase pause rule will apply to:

____

My default grocery/shopping strategy will be:

____

And tired is real. A system that only works when you feel motivated is not a system—it's a wish. This builds a personal operating system.

The third way to remove overwhelm is to build **quick wins** into your plan. Quick wins create dopamine, and dopamine fuels continued effort. Paying off one small balance. Saving your first $500. Cancelling three subscriptions and redirecting that money. These wins are not childish—they are neurological strategy. The brain needs evidence that the effort is working. When it sees wins, it wants more wins.

Quick Wins Momentum List

Three quick financial wins I can achieve in the next 14 days:

1. ____________________
2. ____________________
3. ____________________

The fastest win I can complete this week is:

____

When I complete it, I will immediately redirect that

momentum toward: ____________________

This helps you stop waiting for "big success" before feeling successful.

Finally, overwhelm is defeated when you stop measuring yourself by perfection and start measuring yourself by progress. Progress is a direction, not a performance.

Progress Over Perfection Reframe

Where have I been expecting perfection from myself financially?

Where have I already made progress that I have not celebrated?

What would it look like for me to measure progress more honestly this month?

This restores emotional stability and self-trust. Scripture puts it simply: *"God is not the author of confusion, but of peace."* (1 Corinthians 14:33). Peace comes when you know what to do next. And that's what FPS gives you: the next right step—clearly.

Now that you have a clear action rhythm and you've learned how to remove overwhelm, it's time to install the most motivating tool in the entire journey: **milestones**. Because milestones don't just track progress—they celebrate it. They turn long journeys into short wins, and short wins into unstoppable momentum.

End-of-Chapter Action Plan

My big goal is: ____________________

My Big 3 for the next 30 days are:

1. ____________________
2. ____________________
3. ____________________

My weekly check-in day is: ____________________

My first quick win is: ____________________

My next right step is: ____________________

In the next chapter, we'll build your milestone system and show you how to track progress in a way that keeps you encouraged, focused, and resilient.

You're no longer carrying the whole journey in your head.
You're walking it—step by step—with confidence.

Chapter 14: Milestones, Tracking, and Adjustments

Progress that isn't measured gets misunderstood—and misunderstood progress often gets abandoned.

One of the greatest threats to financial success isn't lack of income or even lack of knowledge. It's discouragement. Discouragement is the silent thief that convinces people the plan "isn't working" when, in reality, the plan is working—just slower than their emotions want. This chapter exists to protect your momentum by teaching you how to track progress in a way that fuels hope instead of draining it.

Milestones and tracking are not about becoming obsessed with numbers. They are about creating **proof**. Proof that you're moving. Proof that your discipline matters. Proof that your future is changing. And once you have proof, motivation becomes internal—because you can literally see your life getting better.

Progress Proof Inventory

In the last 30–90 days, what financial improvements have I already made?

What habits have improved, even if my numbers are not where I want them yet?

What would I overlook if I only measured my balance and ignored my behavior?

Measuring Progress Without Discouragement

Progress becomes discouraging when people measure the wrong thing—or measure the right thing the wrong way. For example, someone might pay $800 toward debt in a month but feel discouraged because the balance "still looks high." Or they may start saving, but feel like the amount is "too small." The issue isn't lack of progress—it's lack of perspective. That's why we track multiple indicators, not just one.

The first key to measuring progress without discouragement is to track **leading indicators** and **lagging indicators**. Lagging indicators are results you see after consistent behavior—like a lower debt balance, a higher credit score, or a growing savings account. Leading indicators are the behaviors that produce those results—like staying within spending limits, making on-time payments, lowering utilization, and holding weekly money meetings. When you track leading indicators, you win more often, because you can celebrate consistency even before the big results appear.

Leading vs. Lagging Indicators Tracker

Below is a simple chart that gives you some key indicators and you have to determine whether you are leading or lagging in that area. You can also add other key indicators that you may want to track.

Indicators	Leading	Lagging
On-time payments	☐	☐
No impulse purchases	☐	☐
Spending within plan	☐	☐
Weekly money meetings	☐	☐
Debt balance decreasing	☐	☐
Extra debt payment made	☐	☐
Savings transfer completed	☐	☐
Savings balance increasing	☐	☐
Credit score improving	☐	☐
Utilization falling	☐	☐
Stress level dropping	☐	☐
	☐	☐
	☐	☐

Which leading indicator, if I stayed consistent with it, would change my life the most?

The second key is to measure progress in **milestones**, not mountains. A mountain feels intimidating because it's one huge goal. A milestone breaks that goal into wins. Instead of "pay off $18,000," you track "first $1,000," "first card paid off," "debt down 25%," "utilization under 50%," "savings hits $500," then "$1,000," then "one month of expenses." Your brain needs wins along the way. Wins create dopamine, and dopamine creates drive.

Milestones, Not Mountains Worksheet

This turns large goals into visible checkpoints.

My large financial goal is: ____________________

My next 5 milestones are:

Examples could include:

- *First $500 saved*
- *First $1,000 debt reduction*
- *First account paid off*
- *Utilization under 50%*
- *One month with no late fees*

1. ____________________
2. ____________________
3. ____________________
4. ____________________
5. ____________________

Now ask yourself:

Which milestone can I hit the fastest? ____________________

Which milestone would build the most confidence?

____

The third key is to track progress visually and consistently. Use simple trackers: a debt thermometer chart, a savings bar, a monthly dashboard, or a checklist of wins. Visual evidence does something powerful to the mind: it transforms hope into certainty.

Visual Tracking Selection Tool

The tracker I will use for debt:

- ☐ Debt thermometer
- ☐ Savings bar
- ☐ Checklist
- ☐ Calendar streak tracker
- ☐ Monthly dashboard

The tracker I will use for savings:

- ☐ Debt thermometer
- ☐ Savings bar
- ☐ Checklist
- ☐ Calendar streak tracker
- ☐ Monthly dashboard

The tracker I will use for habits:

- ☐ Debt thermometer
- ☐ Savings bar
- ☐ Checklist
- ☐ Calendar streak tracker
- ☐ Monthly dashboard

Where will I keep this tracker so I see it regularly?

This makes tracking practical, not theoretical.

Every checkmark becomes proof that you're not the same person you used to be. And scripture supports this kind of steady, encouraged movement: *"Let us not grow weary in doing good, for in due season we shall reap, if we do not lose heart."* (Galatians 6:9). "Due season" requires tracking so you don't quit early.

Finally, understand this: discouragement often comes from comparing your timeline to someone else's. Your progress is your progress. If you're moving forward, you're winning. Even a slow decrease in debt is still the elimination of bondage. Even small savings is still preparation. Progress is not about speed alone—it's about direction and consistency. When you measure correctly, you realize you're closer than you feel.

Comparison Detox Reflection

This is important because discouragement often comes from comparison.

Whose financial timeline am I tempted to compare myself to?

How has comparison distorted my view of my own progress?

What evidence proves that I am moving forward, even if my pace is slower than I hoped?

Course-Correcting Without Quitting

One of the most powerful features of a GPS is rerouting. The GPS doesn't shame you for a wrong turn. It doesn't accuse you of failure. It simply recalculates and says, "Here's the new best route." That is exactly how your financial journey should work. A setback isn't a sign to quit—it's a sign to adjust.

Reroute, Don't Quit Audit

My recent setback was: ____________________

What changed?

☐ Income decreased
☐ Emergency happened
☐ Expenses rose
☐ Discipline slipped
☐ Other: __________________________

What is this setback teaching me?

What is the next best route from here?

Most people quit because they interpret disruption as defeat. A surprise expense, a medical bill, a slow month at work, or an emergency repair happens—and they assume the plan is broken. But the plan isn't broken. Life happened. And the purpose of a system is not to prevent life—it's to help you navigate life without losing momentum.

Course-correcting starts with identifying what changed. Did income decrease? Did an emergency happen? Did expenses rise? Did discipline slip? Then you respond with a specific adjustment—not a vague promise. That might mean temporarily reducing your extra debt payment, switching to minimums for one month to rebuild cash, pausing discretionary spending for two weeks, or selling unused items to close the gap. The goal is to keep moving, even if the speed changes.

Setback Response Plan

If income drops, I will: ______________________________

If an emergency expense happens, I will: ________________

____

If I miss a goal this month, I will: ___________________

If I overspend, I will: ________________________________

What adjustment can I make immediately without quitting the plan entirely?

____

This builds resilience before the next setback arrives.

Another key to course correction is removing shame. Shame makes people hide. Hiding makes problems grow. But when you treat setbacks like data, you stay empowered.

Shame-to-Strategy Reframe

What setback have I been treating like failure?

____

If I looked at it as information instead of shame, what would it tell me?

___

What system needs strengthening because of this setback?

- ☐ Emergency fund
- ☐ Spending buffer
- ☐ Automation
- ☐ Income increase
- ☐ Planning rhythm
- ☐ Other: ____________________

A setback is information: it shows where your plan needs strengthening—maybe a bigger emergency fund, more buffer in variable spending, or more automation. In that sense, setbacks are not interruptions; they are upgrades.

Scripture reinforces persistence with wisdom: *"Though the righteous fall seven times, they rise again."* (Proverbs 24:16). The victory isn't never falling—it's rising.

Rise Again Declaration

When setbacks happen, I will no longer say: ____________

____

Instead, I will say: ______________________________

I am still a builder because: ________________________

The next action that proves I am still moving is: __________

____

The goal of FPS is not flawless execution; it's resilient execution. Course-correcting is how you rise. It's how you keep your identity as a builder even in a difficult season.

Now that you know how to track progress with encouragement and adjust without quitting, it's time to prepare for the challenges that test every financial journey: unexpected obstacles, emergencies, and pressure moments that tempt you to go back to old habits.

End-of-Chapter Milestone Review

One proof of progress I will celebrate this week: __________

____

One milestone I am currently pursuing: ________________

____

One adjustment I need to make right now: ______________

____

One reason I will not quit: ___________________________

____

In the next chapter, we'll talk about navigating setbacks without losing momentum—and how to create a "detour plan" that protects your progress when life hits.

You're not just learning to manage money. You're learning to stay the course—no matter what.

Chapter 15: Navigating Financial Obstacles

Life doesn't cancel your progress—unless you interpret obstacles as failure.

If you stay on this journey long enough, you will face obstacles. Not because you're doing something wrong, but because life is life. Tires go flat. Kids need things. Hours get cut. Unexpected medical bills appear. Someone gets laid off. A major appliance breaks at the worst possible time. These moments don't mean you're failing—they mean you're human and you're living in the real world.

This chapter is designed to do one thing: keep you from losing your momentum when life hits you. The Financial Progression System isn't built for perfect people in perfect seasons. It's built for real people navigating real responsibilities. Your success isn't determined by whether obstacles come—it's determined by whether you know how to respond when they do.

Obstacle Mindset Reset

A financial obstacle I have faced before is: ____________________

____

When obstacles happen, I usually tell myself: ________________

____

A healthier belief I need to adopt is: ________________________

____

An obstacle is not proof I am failing. It is proof I need a response.

Emergencies, Setbacks, and Detours

An emergency is an unexpected event that requires immediate money. A setback is a disruption that slows your progress. A detour is a temporary change in route that still leads you toward the destination. Understanding these differences matters because many people label everything as a "financial disaster," and that emotional labeling triggers panic spending, quitting, or avoidance.

Emergency, Setback, or Detour Classifier

What happened?	Emergency	Setback	Detour
Car repair	☐	☐	☐
Slow work month	☐	☐	☐
Medical copay	☐	☐	☐
Unexpected school expense	☐	☐	☐
Appliance replacement	☐	☐	☐
Reduced overtime	☐	☐	☐
	☐	☐	☐
	☐	☐	☐

What recent financial challenge have I mislabeled as a disaster?

This reduces emotional exaggeration.

Emergencies are inevitable. The goal is not to avoid them; the goal is to be prepared for them so they don't knock you back into debt. This is why the emergency fund is not optional—it is your financial shock absorber.

Emergency Fund Reality Check

My current emergency fund balance is: $__________

My first emergency fund target is: $______________

My next emergency fund target is: $______________

If an emergency happened this month, how would I currently pay for it?

- ☐ Savings
- ☐ Credit card
- ☐ Borrowing
- ☐ Payment plan
- ☐ Other: ________________________

What is one action I can take this month to strengthen my financial shock absorber?

This moves you toward preparedness.

Without it, emergencies get financed with credit cards, personal loans, or payday advances, and the cycle repeats. With it, an emergency becomes an inconvenience you handle—not a crisis that owns you.

Setbacks often come from timing issues: a slower income month, an unplanned expense, or a season where your financial energy is stretched thin. The danger of setbacks isn't the setback itself—it's the story you tell yourself about it. Many people interpret setbacks as proof they'll "never get ahead." That thought becomes discouragement, discouragement becomes avoidance, and avoidance becomes financial drift. Setbacks don't destroy plans—discouragement does.

Setback Story Audit

A setback I experienced was: ______________________________

The story I told myself about it was: ________________________

____

Was that story true, exaggerated, or fear-based?

____

What is a wiser interpretation of that setback?

____

Detours are different. A detour is when you intentionally adjust your plan without abandoning it. You might reduce extra debt payments temporarily, pause a savings goal for 30 days, or shift spending categories to absorb a new expense. A detour is not a quit—it's a strategy. And here's the dopamine shift: when you learn to treat obstacles as detours instead of dead ends, you stop fearing life. You stop feeling fragile. You begin to feel powerful.

Detour, Not Dead End Reframe

A current obstacle I am facing is: ________________________

How I first interpreted it: _____________________________

How I can now see it as a detour: ________________________

If this is a detour, what route adjustment is needed?

Scripture gives perspective that fits this perfectly: *"In this world you will have trouble. But take heart; I have overcome the world."* (John 16:33). Trouble is expected. What changes is your response. When you build your plan with resilience, trouble becomes something you navigate—not something that defeats you.

How to Reroute Instead of Restarting

A GPS doesn't start the trip over because you missed a turn. It recalculates. That is the mindset of financial maturity: **reroute, don't restart**. Restarting is what people do when they fall into shame. Rerouting is what people do when they stay in wisdom.

The first step to rerouting is to pause and assess without emotion.

Pause and Assess Worksheet

What happened? ______________________________

How much will it cost? $__________

When does it need to be handled? ____________________

Is this a true emergency or simply unexpected?

☐ true emergency ☐ simply unexpected

What are my options? ___________________________

What is the wisest next move?

This step matters because panic makes people overreact financially—using high-interest debt, making impulsive choices, or draining savings unnecessarily. Assessment brings calm back into the process, and calm leads to better decisions.

The second step is to activate your "detour budget." A detour budget is a pre-planned category for unexpected expenses—small emergencies, repairs, medical copays, and surprise obligations. If you don't have one yet, you can create it immediately by redirecting money leaks, cutting one or two variable categories temporarily, or using a small portion of savings strategically. The goal is to cover the obstacle without destroying the entire plan.

My Detour Budget Builder

My current detour budget amount is: $__________

If I do not have one, I can create one by:

Reducing: ____________________

Pausing: ____________________

Redirecting: ____________________

Using from savings strategically: ________________

My target detour budget amount is: $____________

The third step is to protect your "non-negotiables." Even in a detour season, there are a few actions you keep consistent—like paying minimums on time, avoiding new debt, and maintaining a weekly money check-in. Non-negotiables keep your identity intact. They keep you from slipping back into avoidance. And they keep your progress alive even when your speed is reduced.

Non-Negotiables Protection Plan

Even during a difficult season, I will still:

Options might include:

Pay minimums on time
Avoid new debt
Review money weekly
Track spending
Communicate with spouse/family
Protect emergency savings from unnecessary use

1. ______________________________
2. ______________________________
3. ______________________________

Which non-negotiable protects my progress the most?

____

The fourth step is to recalibrate the timeline, not the destination. If you were paying $400 extra toward debt and now can only do $150 for two months, that's okay. You didn't fail—you adjusted. The destination remains debt freedom. The ETA changes slightly.

Timeline Recalibration Tool

Before this obstacle, my target timeline was:

____

Because of this detour, my revised timeline is:

____

What changed? ____________________

What did not change? ____________________

Is the destination still the same? ☐ Yes ☐No

What helps me remember that a slower route is still a successful route?

What destroys people isn't timeline change—it's quitting. Scripture encourages this kind of steadfastness: *"A righteous person may fall seven times and rise again."* (Proverbs 24:16). Rising again is rerouting.

Finally, once the obstacle passes, you return to your original route with confidence. And here's what's powerful: every reroute builds resilience.

A financial obstacle I have already survived is:

What did that experience prove about me?

How am I stronger now than I was before?

What part of my system is stronger because of this challenge?

This builds self-trust.

You start trusting yourself because you realize you can handle life without collapsing financially. Your system becomes stronger. Your mindset becomes steadier. And your progress becomes more sustainable than it ever was before.

You now have a strategy for obstacles, setbacks, and detours. You are no longer the person who quits when life gets real. You are becoming the person who recalculates and keeps moving.

My Obstacle Response Plan

When a financial obstacle happens, I will:

1. Pause and assess
2. Classify it correctly
3. Use or build my detour budget
4. Protect my non-negotiables
5. Recalibrate my timeline
6. Resume the route with confidence

The next obstacle I face, I will respond by:

This creates a ready-made response system.

End-of-Chapter Identity Declaration

I am no longer the person who quits when life gets difficult. I am becoming the person who recalculates, responds, and keeps moving.

My current detour is: ____________________________

My next right step is: ____________________________

My reason for continuing is: ____________________

In the next part of FPS, we shift into a new dimension of acceleration: **Choosing Your Mode of Travel**—the strategies, habits, and mindset shifts that increase your speed without sacrificing sustainability.

You've learned how to survive detours.
Now you're going to learn how to accelerate on purpose.

PART V – CHOOSING YOUR MODE OF TRAVEL

How you move financially determines how fast—and how far—you go.

Your destination matters—but so does your vehicle. In the Financial Progression System, your "mode of travel" is how you generate money and momentum. Some people try to reach financial freedom in a slow vehicle with no engine—depending on hope, minimum payments, and occasional motivation. But the truth is, speed and sustainability come from choosing the right income vehicle for your season, your skills, and your goals.

This part is not about becoming a workaholic. It's about becoming intentional. You will learn how the four primary income vehicles work, what they're best for, what their risks are, and how to use them strategically—so your financial journey accelerates without burning you out. Think of this as upgrading your vehicle, strengthening your engine, and making sure you have enough fuel to go the distance.

Chapter 16: Income Vehicles

Employment

Employment is the most common income vehicle, and for many people, it's the most stable starting point. A job provides predictable income, often includes benefits, and can support a consistent debt payoff and savings plan. Employment is not "less than" entrepreneurship—it is a powerful tool when used wisely. It is the foundation that can fund your goals while you build other income streams.

My Current Income Vehicle Snapshot

My current primary income vehicle is:

- ☐ Employment
- ☐ Entrepreneurship
- ☐ Side Income
- ☐ Passive Income

My current monthly income from this vehicle is: $________

How stable is this income right now?

- ☐Very stable
- ☐Somewhat stable
- ☐Unstable

How dependent is my financial plan on this one vehicle?

____

The key to maximizing employment is not just earning a paycheck—it's leveraging the full compensation package. That means understanding benefits like 401(k) matching, health insurance, HSA options, tuition reimbursement, and overtime opportunities. Many people ignore benefits because they don't feel like "income," but benefits are financial leverage.

Employment Optimization Audit

Do I fully understand my compensation package?
☐Yes ☐ No

Benefits I currently use:

401(k) match:	☐Yes ☐ No
Health insurance:	☐Yes ☐ No
HSA/FSA:	☐Yes ☐ No
Tuition reimbursement:	☐Yes ☐ No
Overtime opportunities:	☐Yes ☐ No
Bonuses/incentives:	☐Yes ☐ No

One benefit I am currently underusing is:

____

One action I can take to increase the value of my

employment this month is: ___________________________

If your employer matches retirement contributions, that is essentially free money. If you have access to lower-cost insurance, that is money saved monthly that can be redirected toward your goals.

Employment also becomes more powerful when you treat your career like an asset. Skills are currency. The more valuable your skillset, the more negotiating power you have. That can mean getting certifications, developing leadership ability, or moving into higher-paying roles. A job isn't just a place you go—it's a platform you can use strategically to increase your income without increasing your stress.

Career as an Asset Builder

The top skill I am paid for right now is: ________________

The next skill that would increase my earning power is:

____

A certification, training, or promotion path I should pursue is: ____

If I increased my income through employment, it would help me: ____

This reframes career growth as financial strategy.

A scripture that fits this mindset without pressure is: *"Do you see a man skilled in his work? He will stand before kings…"* (Proverbs 22:29). Skill increases access. And access increases income. When employment is used with intention—budgeting, skill-building, and benefits optimization—it becomes a stable vehicle that can carry you far.

Entrepreneurship

Entrepreneurship is the income vehicle built for expansion. It offers the potential for high income, flexibility, and wealth building—but it also comes with risk, responsibility, and the need for discipline. Entrepreneurship is not for impulsive people looking for quick money. It is for builders who are willing to learn, serve, and stay consistent long enough for results to compound.

Entrepreneurship Fit Test

I want entrepreneurship because: ____________________

Am I willing to:

Solve a real problem consistently? ☐Yes ☐ No
Start lean? ☐Yes ☐ No
Track expenses and revenue? ☐Yes ☐ No
Learn before scaling? ☐Yes ☐ No
Be patient with results? ☐Yes ☐ No

The problem I may be able to solve for profit is:

____

This helps assess readiness instead of impulse.

The biggest misunderstanding about entrepreneurship is that it's just about "having a business." In reality, entrepreneurship is problem-solving for profit. The more clearly you solve a real problem, the more valuable your business becomes.

Business Idea Validation Sheet

The problem I want to solve is: ____________________

The person I want to solve it for is: ________________

The solution I could offer is: ______________________

How people currently solve this problem:

____

Why my solution could be valuable: _________________

The simplest version I could test in the next 30 days is:

____

____

This causes clarity and keeps the business idea grounded.

Whether you provide a service, sell a product, coach, consult, or build something digital, the goal is the same: create value people are willing to pay for consistently.

Entrepreneurship becomes sustainable when you start smart. Many people fail because they start big—big expenses, big expectations, and no systems. FPS teaches you to start lean: validate the idea, generate revenue early, track expenses, and build structure before scaling. You don't need perfection—you need consistency and cash flow.

Start Lean Business Plan

This is the execution worksheet for entrepreneurs.

My business idea: ________________________________

My startup cost limit: $___________

My first offer: __________________________________

My first revenue target: $__________

My first customer source: _________________________

What system must I build first? ____________________

Do this and prevent costly overbuilding. If your business doesn't produce profit or predictable income, it becomes a hobby that drains your financial plan instead of accelerating it.

Scripture supports entrepreneurial stewardship with balance: *"Commit your work to the Lord, and your plans will be established."* (Proverbs 16:3). Entrepreneurship is not just hustle—it's intentional building. When done with wisdom, it can become one of the fastest vehicles toward debt freedom, wealth, and legacy.

Side Income

Side income is the bridge between where you are and where you want to be. It's the extra stream that can shorten debt payoff timelines, increase savings, and create breathing room without requiring you to quit your job or take huge risks. Side income is often the most practical accelerator for people who want progress quickly.

Side Income Strategy Builder

A side income that fits my schedule is: ____________________

A side income that fits my skills is: ________________________

A side income that could start fastest is: __________________

Hours I can realistically give weekly: _________

My weekly side income goal is: $_________

Side income can come from freelance work, gig platforms, selling services, tutoring, consulting, delivery driving, cleaning services, virtual assistance, or selling digital products. The key is choosing something that fits your schedule, energy, and skills. Side income works best when it is structured—meaning you set a weekly income target, schedule the hours, and track where the money goes. Without structure, side income becomes inconsistent and doesn't create lasting progress.

One of the best uses of side income is strategic assignment. For example: "All side income goes to debt until the credit cards are gone." Or: "All side income goes to building a $2,000 emergency fund." When side income has a mission, it becomes exciting.

Side Income Assignment Plan

Every dollar of side income will be assigned to:

☐ Debt
☐ Emergency Fund
☐ Savings

☐ Investment
☐ Business seed money

My side income mission is: ______________________

My side income target amount is: $__________

When I hit this amount, I will redirect the money toward:

____

This gives your side income a job and a purpose.

You can literally watch a side income change your life. It gives you the sense of acceleration, like switching lanes on the highway and feeling the car move forward faster.

Scripture supports the idea of increasing through diligence: *"Lazy hands make for poverty, but diligent hands bring wealth."* (Proverbs 10:4). Side income is diligent hands in motion. Not forever—but for a season. And if you commit to it strategically, it can compress years of struggle into months of progress.

Passive Income

Passive income is the wealth vehicle. It's income that continues with limited ongoing effort after it is built. The truth is, most passive income is not "passive" at the start—it requires upfront work, capital, learning, or systems. But once established, it becomes the kind of income that frees time, reduces stress, and fuels long-term financial stability.

Passive Income Readiness Reflection

When I hear "passive income," I usually think of:

____

What asset could I realistically begin building?

____

Do I currently have more time, money, or knowledge to invest? ____

What passive income vehicle fits my current season best?

____

This keeps expectations realistic and strategic.

Passive income can include rental income, dividend investments, interest-bearing accounts, digital products, affiliate income, royalties, and automated business systems. The key is building assets that pay you. Debt freedom is important, but wealth is created through assets. Passive income is how you move from being paid only when you work to being paid because you own something valuable.

Asset-Building Plan

The first asset I want to build is: ____________________

Why this asset matters to me: ______________________

What it will require upfront:

☐ Time
☐ Money
☐ Skills
☐ Systems

The first step to building this asset is: ____________________

My target date to begin is: ____________________

This makes passive income actionable.

The reason passive income matters so much is because it changes your relationship with time. Employment and side income are often time-for-money exchanges. Passive income begins to disconnect income from hours. That's when freedom becomes real. You can take a day off and still earn. You can sleep and still earn. You can age and still earn. Passive income is not just about money—it's about sustainability.

Scripture hints at this principle through wisdom and multiplication: *"Cast your bread upon the waters, for you will find it after many days."* (Ecclesiastes 11:1). That is the idea of investing—placing resources wisely and receiving return later. Passive income is delayed gratification turned into a system. And once you begin building it, your future starts gaining momentum that doesn't rely solely on your labor.

Now that you understand the four income vehicles—

The Income Vehicle Comparison Chart

Income Vehicle	My Current Level	Best Benefit	Best Use Right Now
Employment		Stability	
Entrepreneurship		Expansion	
Side Income		Acceleration	
Passive Income		Wealth	

Which vehicle is my current foundation? ________________

Which vehicle is my next growth move? ________________

Which vehicle do I need to learn more about? ____________

The next chapter will help you choose your best combination based on your personality, your risk tolerance, and your season of life. Because the goal is not to do everything. The goal is to do what fits—consistently—and build forward with confidence.

You've chosen a destination.
Now you're choosing the vehicle that can actually get you there—faster, safer, and stronger.

Chapter 17: Risk Tolerance & Financial Personality

The best financial strategy is the one you can follow without fear, burnout, or self-sabotage.

One of the biggest reasons people fail financially is not because they chose a "bad" strategy—it's because they chose a strategy that didn't match **who they are**. They followed someone else's blueprint, tried to move at someone else's speed, or adopted a plan that required a personality they don't naturally have. That mismatch creates stress, inconsistency, and eventually quitting.

This chapter is about alignment. When your strategy matches your temperament, money becomes easier to manage. Your plan feels sustainable instead of suffocating. Your decisions become calmer because they fit your natural wiring. And when you move in a way that fits you, progress becomes steady—and steady progress builds unstoppable confidence.

Financial Personality Snapshot

When it comes to money, I naturally tend to be more:

☐ Cautious
☐ Bold
☐ Mixed

When pressure rises, I usually:

☐ Slow down and protect
☐ Push harder and act
☐ Avoid
☐ Overthink

When making financial decisions, I rely most on:

- ☐ Logic
- ☐ Emotion
- ☐ Speed
- ☐ Research
- ☐ Other people's opinions

My biggest money strength is: ___________________

My biggest money weakness is: ___________________

Conservative vs. Aggressive Strategies

A conservative strategy prioritizes safety, stability, and predictability. Conservative people tend to value peace of mind, consistent routines, and low financial surprises. They prefer solid plans over risky opportunities, and they often feel better when they have savings in place before making big moves. Conservative strategies aren't "slow"—they're **stable**, and stability is a form of strength.

If you're conservative, the smartest approach usually includes building an emergency fund early, using debt payoff methods that reduce stress, avoiding high-interest borrowing, and investing consistently over time rather than trying to "time the market." You may also prefer stable income vehicles like employment or structured side income with predictable hours. Conservative strategies work best when they focus on consistency, automation, and protecting progress from emotional swings.

An aggressive strategy prioritizes speed, growth, and leverage. Aggressive people tend to be opportunity-driven. They are willing to move fast, take calculated risks, and endure temporary discomfort for long-term gain. They often get energized by challenges, growth goals, and the possibility of scaling income quickly. When aggressive strategies are guided by wisdom, they can compress timelines dramatically.

Aggressive strategies often include aggressive debt payoff plans, income expansion through entrepreneurship, investing earlier, and pursuing opportunities like business building, commissions, or performance-based income. Aggressive movers tend to do well with goals that feel like missions: "Pay off $15,000 in 9 months," "Increase income by $2,000/month," or "Build a second stream by summer." The danger is not aggression—it's aggression without structure. Without a plan, aggressive people can overextend, over borrow, or chase too many things at once.

Scripture gives balance that applies perfectly here: *"The prudent see danger and take refuge…"* (Proverbs 22:3) and also, *"Be strong and courageous…"* (Joshua 1:9). Prudence represents healthy caution. Courage represents healthy boldness. The goal is not to be conservative or aggressive—it's to be **wise**.

Conservative vs. Aggressive Strategy Assessment

I relate more to Conservative:	I relate more to Aggressive:
I value stability	I like speed
I like clear plans	I am energized by opportunity
I want savings before risk	I can tolerate uncertainty
I dislike surprises	I like bold goals
I prefer predictable income	I prefer growth over comfort

Which side sounds more like me right now? ______________

Which side has hurt me in the past when left unchecked?

____

My Wise Strategy Choice

My natural financial style is: ___________________________

The strengths of this style are: _________________________

The dangers of this style are: __________________________

To stay wise, I must remember to: _____________________

Wisdom knows when to protect and when to pursue.

Matching Tools to Temperament

Your temperament is how you naturally respond to pressure, uncertainty, and decision-making. Some people feel calm when they have detailed plans. Others feel energized by flexibility and big goals. Some people hate risk. Others hate boredom.

Temperament Under Pressure Audit

When money gets tight, I tend to:

When I feel behind financially, I tend to:

When I get extra money, I tend to:

When I feel excited about an opportunity, I tend to:

___

If you ignore temperament, you will choose tools that you don't use consistently—and unused tools don't produce results.

Matching Tools to My Temperament

Tools that calm me and make me consistent:

___

___

Tools that motivate me and create momentum:

___

___

Tools I avoid even though they are "good" tools:

___

___

Why do I avoid them?

___

For example, conservative personalities tend to thrive with tools like automation, sinking funds, clear budgets, stable investments, and step-by-step debt payoff methods that create frequent reassurance. They do well with "guardrail" systems: caps on variable spending, a weekly money meeting, and clear rules like "no new debt" or "cash-only for discretionary spending." These tools lower anxiety and increase confidence.

Aggressive personalities tend to thrive with tools that create acceleration: income expansion plans, side income targets, entrepreneurship goals, investment automation, and milestone-based challenges. They do well with scoreboards: dashboards, progress trackers, and "30-day sprints." However, aggressive personalities must build in protection tools too—like emergency funds, risk limits, and accountability—because speed without guardrails can lead to crashes.

Guardrails for My Personality

Because of my personality, I need these financial guardrails: Examples: *No new debt, Emergency fund minimum, 24-hour pause before big purchases, Weekly review, Accountability partner, Monthly spending cap*

1. ____________________
2. ____________________
3. ____________________

Which guardrail would protect me the most right now?

____

There are also temperament traits beyond conservative/aggressive. Some people are planners; others are spontaneous. Some are detail-oriented; others are big-picture.

Some are emotionally driven; others are logic-driven. A planner should use budgets, calendars, automation, and clear milestones. A spontaneous person should use simplified systems: fewer categories, spending limits, and "container" methods like separate accounts for bills, spending, and saving. The goal is not to change your personality—it's to create a system that works **with** it.

Planner, Spontaneous, Detail-Oriented, or Big-Picture?

I am more:

- ☐ Planner
- ☐ Spontaneous
- ☐ Detail-oriented
- ☐ Big-picture
- ☐ Mixed

Because of that, I should use: ______________________

Examples:
Planner - calendars, milestones, budget templates
Spontaneous - fewer categories, spending caps, separate accounts
Detail-oriented - trackers, dashboards, checklists
Big-picture - simple scoreboards, goal boards, monthly targets

What type of system would feel natural enough for me to maintain for 12 months?

Scripture supports this concept of self-awareness and wise building: *"Suppose one of you wants to build a tower. Won't you first sit down and estimate the cost…?"* (Luke 14:28). Estimating cost is about knowing yourself and knowing your reality. When you choose tools that fit your temperament, you stop fighting yourself. And when you stop fighting yourself, momentum becomes natural.

My Financial Fit Blueprint

My financial personality is: ____________________

My risk tolerance is: ____________________

The tools that fit me best are:

1. ____________________
2. ____________________
3. ____________________

The habits that support me best are:

1. ____________________
2. ____________________
3. ____________________

The risks I must protect myself from are:

1. ____________________
2. ____________________
3. ____________________

The Dopamine Shift: Confidence Through Fit

Here's the breakthrough people feel when they match tools to temperament: relief. They stop forcing themselves to be someone else. They stop quitting because the plan felt too strict or too loose. They start winning consistently, and those wins create a healthy dopamine loop: progress → confidence → consistency → more progress.

Relief, Confidence, and Fit Reflection

What financial strategy have I been trying to force that does not fit me?

What kind of relief would I feel if I stopped fighting my natural wiring?

What strategy feels sustainable for me now?

When your strategy fits you, your money stops feeling like a battlefield. It starts feeling like a blueprint. And once that happens, you'll notice something powerful: you're not just building wealth—you're building self-trust.

Now that you understand your risk tolerance and financial personality, it's time to put that self-awareness to work by building the habits that accelerate wealth—without burnout and without relapse.

End-of-Chapter Financial Personality Action Plan

My financial personality is: ____________________

My risk style is: ______________________________

My best-fit tools are: __________________________

My needed guardrails are: ______________________

The one system I will begin using immediately is:

In the next chapter, we'll focus on the practical habits and systems that make progress automatic, consistent, and scalable.

You've learned how you move best.
Now you're going to build habits that keep you moving—faster and farther.

Chapter 18: Habits That Accelerate Wealth

Wealth isn't built by luck—it's built by repeatable habits that run even when motivation fades.

At this point in the Financial Progression System, you've done what most people never do: you located your starting point, chose your destination, built a route, and selected your mode of travel. Now comes the secret weapon that determines whether you arrive early or arrive exhausted: **habits**. Not hype. Not inspiration. Habits.

My Current Wealth Habit Audit

My strongest financial habit right now is: ________________

My weakest financial habit right now is: ________________

One habit helping me move forward is: ________________

One habit quietly slowing me down is: ________________

If I improved one habit in the next 30 days, which one would change my life the most? ______________________________

Habits are powerful because they remove daily negotiations. They turn financial success into something you do automatically instead of something you constantly struggle to do. This chapter is designed to create a healthy momentum loop in your life—where progress creates excitement, excitement fuels consistency, and consistency produces results you can feel in your bank account and in your peace.

Automation

Automation is one of the most overlooked wealth accelerators because it doesn't feel exciting at first. But automation is what separates people who "try" to do the right thing from people who **consistently** do the right thing. Automation is a decision you make once that pays you back repeatedly—like setting your finances on cruise control while still keeping your hands on the wheel.

One Decision, Repeated Payoff

One financial decision I can make once and benefit from repeatedly is: ________________________________

This decision will protect:

- ☐My time
- ☐My payment history
- ☐My savings
- ☐My debt payoff
- ☐My peace

The reason I have delayed this decision is: ____________

____

What would change if I set it up this week? ____________

____

The first purpose of automation is protection. Human beings get tired. We forget. We get distracted. We get emotional. Automation keeps your plan moving even when your emotions are loud. Automatic bill pay protects your payment history. Automatic debt payments protect your payoff timeline. Automatic savings transfers protect your future. Automation is not laziness—it's wisdom.

Automation Setup Checklist

I have automated:

Bills:	☐ Yes ☐ No
Minimum debt payments:	☐ Yes ☐ No
Savings transfers:	☐ Yes ☐ No
Investing contributions:	☐ Yes ☐ No
Credit monitoring alerts:	☐ Yes ☐ No

The first automation I still need to set up is: ______________

The date I will set it up is: ____________________

This is you admitting, "I don't want my destiny to depend on my mood."

The second purpose of automation is simplicity. Many people fail financially because they carry too many mental responsibilities—remembering due dates, tracking balances, deciding what to pay first. Automation reduces the number of decisions you must make. When fewer decisions are required, you experience less overwhelm, and your follow-through improves. This is especially important in busy seasons where life demands a lot of mental energy.

Simplicity Reduces Overwhelm Builder

The money decisions that drain me most are:

1. ____________________
2. ____________________
3. ____________________

Which of these can be simplified or automated?

____

What recurring decision can I remove from my life this month?

____

The third purpose of automation is acceleration. When you automate savings and investing, you build wealth before you can spend the money impulsively. You pay yourself first. You create momentum quietly, and then one day you look up and realize your savings is bigger, your debt is smaller, and your stress is lower—without needing constant motivation.

Scripture supports this concept of order and consistency: *"Let all things be done decently and in order."* (1 Corinthians 14:40). Automation is financial order. It turns chaos into a system. And once your system is running, your confidence rises because your progress is no longer fragile—it's structured.

Consistency

Consistency is the habit that makes every other habit work. People often assume wealth is built by big moves—big investments, big income jumps, big wins. But most wealth is built by **small actions repeated** over time. Consistency is not glamorous, but it is unstoppable. A small consistent saver will outperform a motivated person who only takes action when they "feel like it." Consistency begins with rhythm, not intensity.

My Consistency Rhythm Plan

A rhythm I can realistically maintain for the next 90 days,

My monthly planning day is: ___________________

My weekly money meeting day is: ___________________

My daily money awareness habit is: ___________________

That means you establish a weekly money meeting, a monthly plan, and daily awareness habits that are realistic for your lifestyle. A 15-minute weekly check-in may not sound life-changing, but it is. It prevents small issues from becoming big emergencies. It keeps you aware of your progress. It helps you stay emotionally connected to your goals. And that emotional connection fuels continued action.

The 15-Minute Weekly Check-In Template

Each week I will review:

- ☐ Current account balance
- ☐ Bills paid / upcoming
- ☐ Spending categories off track
- ☐ Progress on debt/savings goal

One adjustment needed this week: _____________________

This week's money check-in date: ____________________

Consistency also means staying steady in seasons of slow results. Sometimes debt payoff feels slow. Sometimes credit score changes take time. Sometimes income growth is gradual. The temptation in those seasons is to quit, switch plans, or search for shortcuts. But consistency is what turns "slow" into "sure."

Slow Results, Sure Results Reflection

Where am I tempted to quit because results feel slow?

___

What evidence shows that progress is still happening?

___

What habit do I need to keep repeating even if the result is not visible yet?

___

If you keep moving, you keep winning—even when the win isn't visible yet.

This is where scripture becomes encouragement, not pressure: *"Let us not grow weary in doing good, for in due season we shall reap…"* (Galatians 6:9). Due season is the reward of consistency. It's the moment when steady effort turns into visible harvest. The people who reach financial freedom aren't always the smartest—they're often the ones who stayed consistent long enough for results to compound.

Finally, consistency builds identity. You stop being someone who is "trying to get better with money" and become someone who **manages money well**. That identity shift is dopamine-rich because it creates pride, self-respect, and self-trust. And when you trust yourself, you stop self-sabotaging.

Identity Through Repetition Statement

I am no longer just trying to get better with money.

I am becoming someone who: ____________________

Three habits that support this identity are:

1. ____________________
2. ____________________
3. ____________________

Compounding Discipline

Compounding discipline is the ability to stay disciplined long enough for your discipline to start producing exponential results. In the beginning, discipline feels like effort. Later, discipline feels like leverage. At first, extra debt payments feel like sacrifice. Later, being debt-free feels like freedom. At first, saving $25 or $50 feels small. Later, watching your account hit $1,000, $5,000, and $10,000 feels powerful. Compounding discipline is what turns small beginnings into massive outcomes.

Compounding Discipline Tracker

The small discipline I am committing to is: ______________

How often I will do it: __________________

What result it should create over time: __________________

____

If I stay consistent for 3 months, I expect: ______________

____

If I stay consistent for 12 months, I expect: ______________

____

The reason compounding discipline matters is because money compounds—but so do habits. When you consistently pay down debt, you reduce interest, which frees cash flow, which allows bigger payments, which accelerates payoff. When you consistently save, you build buffers, which reduce emergencies, which prevents new debt, which stabilizes progress. When you consistently invest, time and growth begin to work for you. Discipline compounds into speed.

Cause-and-Effect Discipline Map

If I consistently pay an extra $________on debt, then: _____

____

If I consistently save $________, then: __________________

____

If I consistently invest $________, then: _________________

____

If I consistently control lifestyle inflation, then: ___________

____

Which disciplined behavior creates the greatest chain reaction in my life? ________________________________

Compounding discipline also protects you from lifestyle inflation. When income rises, disciplined people don't automatically upgrade everything. They upgrade intentionally. They increase savings, investments, and giving first. They expand their lifestyle second. That order is the difference between people who make more but stay stressed and people who make more and become free.

Lifestyle Inflation Guardrail Plan

My personal rule for income increases is:

Giving: ________%
Savings: ________%
Investing: ________%
Debt payoff: ________%
Lifestyle upgrades: ________%

When my income increases, I will first direct money toward:

____

Scripture captures compounding discipline through the principle of sowing and reaping: *"Whatever a man sows, that he will also reap."* (Galatians 6:7). Your habits are seeds. Your financial outcomes are harvest.

Seeds and Harvest Reflection

The habits I am sowing right now are: ____________________

The financial harvest I want to reap is: ____________________

What seed do I need to stop planting? ____________________

What seed do I need to plant more consistently? __________

____

The more consistently you sow discipline, the more predictable your harvest becomes. And predictability is where peace is born—because your future becomes less of a mystery.

Here's the dopamine moment: once compounding discipline kicks in, progress begins to speed up on its own. Debt drops faster. Savings grows quicker. Confidence increases. Your financial world becomes lighter. And you start craving that feeling—not from spending, but from winning.

My Wealth Acceleration Plan

The automation I will set up first is: ____________________

The consistency rhythm I will protect is: __________________

The discipline I will compound is: _______________________

The habit I will stop immediately is: ____________________

The financial result I am accelerating toward is: ___________

____

You now have the habits that accelerate wealth: automation that protects you, consistency that stabilizes you, and compounding discipline that multiplies your outcomes. Next, we shift into the fuel stations of the journey—your resources.

End-of-Chapter 30-Day Habit Challenge

For the next 30 days, I will:

- ☐ Keep my weekly money meeting
- ☐ Follow my automation plan
- ☐ Repeat my chosen daily habit
- ☐ Track one sign of progress each week

The habit I am building first is: ______________________

Why this matters to my future: ______________________

In the next part of FPS, you will learn how to identify and leverage the internal and external resources that make success easier, faster, and more sustainable.

You're not just moving anymore.
You're accelerating—with structure and purpose.

PART VI – RECOGNIZING YOUR RESOURCES

Resources are the fuel stations on your journey.

A GPS route is only as successful as the fuel available along the way. You can have the best destination and the best strategy, but if you don't recognize your resources, you'll run out of strength before you arrive. Most people think resources are only external—money, connections, and opportunities. But in the Financial Progression System, your greatest resources start inside you.

Internal resources are what keep you steady when life gets loud, when progress feels slow, and when temptation feels strong. They are the invisible strengths that turn a plan into a lifestyle. This chapter is designed to help you identify, develop, and rely on the inner tools that make financial growth sustainable—not just possible.

Chapter 19: Internal Resources

Discipline

Discipline is the resource that keeps your future protected even when your feelings fluctuate. Motivation comes and goes, but discipline remains. Discipline is not a personality trait reserved for certain people—it is a skill that can be built, strengthened, and repeated until it becomes part of your identity. The greatest financial change doesn't come from one big decision; it comes from many disciplined decisions stacked over time.

Exercise: Internal Resource Self-Assessment

When it comes to money, I currently rate myself from 1–10 in:

Discipline:

1	2	3	4	5	6	7	8	9	10

Patience:

1	2	3	4	5	6	7	8	9	10

Confidence:

1	2	3	4	5	6	7	8	9	10

Delayed Gratification:

1	2	3	4	5	6	7	8	9	10

My strongest internal resource right now is: ______________

My weakest internal resource right now is: ______________

Discipline functions like a financial steering wheel. Without it, you drift. With it, you stay on route. It shows up in the small moments: choosing to track expenses, staying within a spending limit, making an extra payment, and resisting impulse buying. The power of discipline is that it doesn't require perfect conditions—it only requires commitment in the conditions you have.

Exercise: Discipline Under Pressure Audit

I tend to lose discipline when I feel:

☐Tired
☐ Stressed
☐ Discouraged
☐ Tempted
☐ Bored
☐ Overwhelmed

The financial habit I struggle most to stay disciplined with is:

____

The situation that most often throws me off course is:

____

What support or structure would help me stay disciplined in that moment?

____

If you want discipline to become dependable, you must stop relying on willpower alone and start building systems that support it. Automation, routines, and boundaries are all discipline multipliers.

Exercise: Discipline Multiplier Builder

One automation that would strengthen my discipline:

____

One routine that would strengthen my discipline:

____

One boundary that would strengthen my discipline:

____

The first multiplier I will install is: ____________________

The date I will begin is: ____________________

The more you remove decision fatigue, the more disciplined you become without feeling exhausted. Discipline becomes sustainable when it is structured.

Scripture gives a balanced view of discipline as training, not punishment: *"Discipline yourself for the purpose of godliness."* (1 Timothy 4:7). In this context, discipline is simply training your life to align with what you value. Financial discipline is training your spending, saving, and planning to match your future. And as discipline grows, you begin to feel something powerful: self-trust. That self-trust becomes fuel.

Patience

Patience is the resource that protects you from quitting in the middle. Most financial plans don't fail because they're wrong—they fail because people become impatient. They want fast results, and when results don't show up quickly, they assume nothing is happening. But financial progress often starts invisibly. Just like the gym, you feel the effort before you see the transformation.

Exercise: Patience Timeline Reflection

One financial area where I feel impatient is: ____________

What result am I hoping to see too quickly? ____________

What evidence shows that progress may still be happening beneath the surface? ______________________________

What would it look like to stay committed for 90 more days?

____

Patience doesn't mean doing nothing. Patience means staying committed while results are forming. It's understanding that debt reduction, credit improvement, and savings growth are processes. The seed is planted before the harvest appears. Patience is what allows you to keep making payments, keep tracking, and keep prioritizing even when the "big win" hasn't arrived yet.

Patience also prevents you from taking shortcuts that cost you long-term peace. Impatience often leads to risky decisions: predatory loans, "get rich quick" schemes, overextending credit, or draining savings too fast. Patience keeps you grounded.

Exercise: Impatience Trap Audit

When I get tired of waiting financially, I am tempted to:

____

The shortcut I am most vulnerable to is: _________________

How has impatience cost me in the past? ________________

____

What wiser long-term choice can I make instead? _________

____

Patience helps you choose steady progress over flashy moves. It's the resource that says, "I'm not rushing into a trap just because I'm tired of the journey."

Scripture frames patience as power: *"Let perseverance finish its work so that you may be mature and complete, lacking nothing."* (James 1:4). Financial maturity requires patience. When you develop patience, you begin to enjoy the process because you understand what it produces. And that understanding removes panic, which makes your decisions sharper.

Financial Confidence

Financial confidence is not arrogance. It's clarity plus repetition. It's knowing what to do, believing you can do it, and watching yourself do it consistently. Financial confidence is one of the most important resources because it changes how you show up. Confident people open bills instead of avoiding them. Confident people check accounts instead of fearing them. Confident people make adjustments instead of giving up.

Confidence grows through evidence. The fastest way to build financial confidence is to create small wins that prove you're capable. Paying off one small debt. Saving your first $500. Going 30 days without overdrafts. Sticking to your spending plan for one week. These wins are not minor—they are identity-building. They train your brain to associate money with control instead of chaos.

Exercise: Small Wins Confidence Builder

Three financial wins I have already achieved:

1. ____
2. ____
3. ____

One recent win that proves I can trust myself more is:

____

The next small win I want to create is: ____________________

____

Financial confidence also reduces stress because it replaces uncertainty with certainty. When you know how to respond to expenses, how to track spending, and how to make strategic decisions, money stops feeling like a mystery. It becomes a system. And systems create peace. The more confident you become, the less reactive you are—and the less reactive you are, the more money you keep.

A gentle scripture that supports confidence is: *"For God has not given us a spirit of fear, but of power, love, and a sound mind."* (2 Timothy 1:7). A sound mind includes financial thinking. As your confidence grows, fear shrinks.

Exercise: Fear vs. Confidence Reframe

A money task I usually avoid is: ________________________

The fear behind that avoidance is: ______________________

What would a confident version of me do instead? ________

____

One action I can take this week to reduce fear is: _________

____

When fear shrinks, your future expands.

Delayed Gratification

Delayed gratification is the internal resource that turns discipline into wealth. It is the ability to choose long-term reward over short-term pleasure. Most people don't struggle because they don't know what to do—they struggle because what they want now competes with what they want most.

Exercise: What I Want Now vs. What I Want Most

What I want now: ______________________________

What I want most: ______________________________

A recent decision where these two competed was: ________

____

Which one did I choose? __________________________

What would alignment look like next time? ____________

____

Delayed gratification is how you win that battle consistently.

This resource is developed through practice, not personality. Start small: wait 24 hours before non-essential purchases. Create a "fun fund" so enjoyment doesn't sabotage goals. Replace impulsive spending with a progress reward—like tracking your debt dropping or savings rising. Over time, delayed gratification becomes easier because your brain starts enjoying the feeling of progress more than the feeling of impulse.

Exercise: Delayed Gratification Practice Plan

One area where I struggle with short-term pleasure is: _____

____

My 24-hour pause rule will apply to: ________________

My "fun fund" amount will be: $________

One impulse I will replace with progress tracking is:

____

Delayed gratification also protects your identity. When you consistently choose your future over your urge, you begin to see yourself differently. You become someone who follows through. Someone who keeps promises to yourself.

Exercise: Promise Keeper Identity Statement

One promise I want to start keeping to myself financially is:

____

The smallest version of that promise I can keep this week is:

____

Keeping this promise will prove that I am becoming someone who: ____

This identity becomes your fuel because you start craving alignment more than consumption.

Scripture supports this long-view thinking: *"Better is the end of a thing than the beginning."* (Ecclesiastes 7:8). The end is the reward: debt freedom, peace, stability, and legacy. Delayed gratification is simply choosing the end over the impulse. And once you experience the end, the journey feels worth it—and you become hungry to go further.

Exercise: My Internal Resource Growth Plan

The internal resource I most need to strengthen is: ________

____

The habit that will help strengthen it is: ________________

The obstacle that weakens it most is: ________________

The support system or structure that will protect it is: ______

____

My first step this week is: __________________________

Now that you've identified your internal resources—discipline, patience, confidence, and delayed gratification—it's time to turn outward and recognize the external resources that can multiply your progress: people, tools, systems, and support.

End-of-Chapter Reflection: What Is Fueling Me Now?

I am no longer relying only on motivation.

I am building my journey on:

Discipline through: __________________________

Patience through: __________________________

Confidence through: __________________________

Delayed gratification through: ____________________

The internal resource I will intentionally practice over the next 30 days is: ________________________________

In the next chapter, we'll cover how to build a support network, leverage mentorship, use technology, and make sure you're not doing this alone.

You're not running on willpower anymore. You're fueling your journey with resources that last.

Chapter 20: External Resources

Your breakthrough doesn't require you to be alone—it requires you to be supported, equipped, and resourced.

A financial journey is not just about what you do—it's also about what you have access to. External resources are the fuel stations that keep you moving when energy is low, when life gets busy, or when obstacles show up unexpectedly. Many people fail not because they lack desire, but because they lack the right support, the right knowledge, and the right systems to stay consistent.

This chapter is about building an environment that makes financial success easier. You are not meant to carry everything in your head or do everything by yourself. When you learn to leverage education, mentors, and practical tools, you stop relying on willpower and start relying on structure. And structure is what turns short-term motivation into long-term results.

Exercise: External Resource Reality Check

Right now, the external resources supporting my financial life are: ____

The areas where I feel under-supported are:

- ☐ Education
- ☐ Mentor

☐ Tools
☐ Accountability
☐ Community
☐ Other ____________________

The kind of support that would help me most right now is:

☐ Education
☐ Mentor
☐ Tools
☐ Accountability
☐ Community
☐ Other ____________________

If I had stronger support, the area of my financial life that would improve fastest is:

☐ Budgeting
☐ Cash Flow
☐ Debt Payoff
☐ Credit
☐ Saving
☐ Investing
☐ Insurance
☐ Legacy Planning

Education

Education is the external resource that replaces confusion with clarity. A lot of financial stress comes from not knowing what to do next. People aren't failing because they're incapable—they're failing because money was never explained to them in a way that made sense. Education gives you language for what you're experiencing, strategy for what you're facing, and confidence for what you're building.

Exercise: Financial Education Gap Finder

The money topics I understand well are:

- ☐ Budgeting
- ☐ Cash Flow
- ☐ Debt Payoff
- ☐ Credit
- ☐ Saving
- ☐ Investing
- ☐ Insurance
- ☐ Legacy Planning
- ☐ Other ________________________

The money topics that still confuse me are:

- ☐ Budgeting
- ☐ Cash Flow
- ☐ Debt Payoff
- ☐ Credit
- ☐ Saving
- ☐ Investing
- ☐ Insurance
- ☐ Legacy Planning
- ☐ Other ________________________

The one area I most need education in right now is:

- ☐ Budgeting
- ☐ Cash Flow
- ☐ Debt Payoff
- ☐ Credit
- ☐ Saving
- ☐ Investing
- ☐ Insurance
- ☐ Legacy Planning
- ☐ Other ______________________

If I gained confidence in this area, what financial decision would become easier? ______________________________

But not all education is equal. Financial education must be practical, applicable, and consistent with your goals. You don't need complicated theories—you need repeatable actions. The best education helps you understand how money works in real life: budgeting, cash flow, debt payoff, credit improvement, saving, investing, insurance, and legacy planning. When education is too abstract, people feel overwhelmed. When education is actionable, people feel empowered.

Exercise: Practical Learning Plan

The financial skill I need to learn next is: ________________

The source I will use to learn it is: _____________________

The day and time I will study it each week is: ____________

The action I will take after learning is: ___________________

This is why structured learning environments matter. A system like FPS—aligned with the Debt Eliminator / Debt Conqueror pathway—does more than teach information. It gives you a step-by-step route that builds skill over time. Education becomes powerful when it's sequential: you learn what to do, apply it, measure results, then move to the next level. That sequence creates momentum and keeps you from jumping around and staying stuck.

Exercise: Sequential Learning Reflection

The last financial topic I learned but did not fully apply was:

____

Why did I stop short of applying it? ___________________

What is the next logical step in my learning path? _________

____

Education also protects you from traps. Many financial setbacks come from believing bad advice, falling for predatory products, or taking shortcuts that cost long-term peace. The more financially educated you become, the harder it is to be manipulated by fear-based marketing and quick-fix promises.

Exercise: Wisdom vs. Noise Filter

Bad financial advice I have believed before: _____________

____

What made it appealing at the time? ___________________

____

How did it cost me peace, money, or progress? __________

____

What standard will I now use to judge financial advice? ____

____

Scripture supports the value of wisdom in a simple, grounded way: *"Wisdom is the principal thing; therefore get wisdom."* (Proverbs 4:7). Wisdom is not just knowledge—it's applied understanding that produces better outcomes.

Mentors

A mentor is a shortcut—with accountability. Mentors don't just give information; they give perspective. They help you avoid mistakes you can't yet see. They help you stay consistent when emotions try to pull you off course. And they can often spot the one adjustment that saves you months of struggle.

Financial mentorship comes in different forms. It can be a coach, a financially stable family member, a trusted advisor, a community leader, or even structured guidance inside a program. The key is not fame—the key is alignment.

Exercise: Mentor Mapping Worksheet

People who could provide healthy financial guidance in my life:

1. ______________________________
2. ______________________________
3. ______________________________

Do they model stability, wisdom, and consistency?

☐Yes ☐ No

The type of mentor I most need right now is:

☐Coach
☐ Accountability partner
☐ Financially stable friend
☐ Structured program
☐ Community leader
☐ Other

The best mentors understand the route you're on and can help you implement it with discipline. A mentor should help you build systems, not dependency. They should teach you how to think, not just what to do.

Exercise: What I Need from a Mentor

What I need most from mentorship right now is:

☐Clarity
☐ Accountability
☐ Encouragement

☐ Strategy
☐ Perspective
☐ Correction

The financial area where I most need guidance is:

☐ Budgeting
☐ Cash Flow
☐ Debt Payoff
☐ Credit
☐ Saving
☐ Investing
☐ Insurance
☐ Legacy Planning
☐ Other ______________________

A good mentor would help me by: ____________________

____

The first step I can take to seek aligned guidance is: _______

____

Mentors also help with mindset. When you're in the middle of paying off debt or rebuilding credit, it's easy to feel like progress is slow or invisible. A mentor reminds you that the process is working. They normalize setbacks and help you reroute without quitting. That emotional reinforcement is powerful because discouragement is one of the biggest reasons people abandon good plans.

Mentorship also raises your standards. When you spend time around people who manage money with intention, your "normal" begins to change. You stop seeing financial stress as inevitable and start seeing it as solvable. And that shift is priceless.

Exercise: Standards Shift Reflection

The financial standard I grew up around was:

☐ **A "taboo" topic:** *never discussed openly*

☐ **A source of constant anxiety:** *frequent talk about bills and lack of money*

☐ **A structured lesson:** *parents actively taught budgeting and saving*

☐ **A "spend while you have it" mindset:** *prioritizing immediate needs over long-term planning*

The financial standard I want to normalize now is:

☐ **Conscious Spending:** *Aligning every dollar spent with personal values rather than social pressure.*

☐ **Financial Peace:** *Choosing low-risk stability over high-stress growth.*

☐ **Generational Wealth:** *Prioritizing assets and legacy over immediate consumption.*

☐ **Radical Transparency:** *Discussing money openly with family and partners to remove stigma.*

☐ **Automated Abundance:** *Setting up systems so saving and investing happen without effort.*

Who in my life reflects the standard I want to build toward?

____

Scripture highlights this principle in a way that fits the moment: *"Plans fail for lack of counsel, but with many advisers they succeed."* (Proverbs 15:22). Counsel doesn't remove your responsibility—it strengthens your execution.

Exercise: Counsel and Accountability Check-In

When I make financial decisions, I usually:

- ☐ Do it alone
- ☐ Ask for advice
- ☐ Avoid asking for help
- ☐ React emotionally

The benefit of wise counsel in my life would be:

____

One financial decision I should stop making in isolation is:

____

Financial Tools and Systems

Tools and systems are what keep you consistent when life gets chaotic. A system is simply a repeatable process that makes the right action easier than the wrong action. Without systems, you rely on memory, motivation, and mental energy. With systems, you rely on structure—and structure wins over emotion.

Exercise: My Current Financial Tools Audit

I currently use these tools:

Budget template:	☐Yes ☐ No
Debt tracker:	☐Yes ☐ No
Savings tracker:	☐Yes ☐ No
Separate bank accounts:	☐Yes ☐ No
Automation:	☐Yes ☐ No
Calendar reminders:	☐Yes ☐ No
Weekly check-in routine:	☐Yes ☐ No
Monthly dashboard:	☐Yes ☐ No

The most helpful tool I already use is: *(choose one)*

☐ Budget template
☐ Debt tracker
☐ Savings tracker
☐ Separate bank accounts
☐ Automation
☐ Calendar reminders
☐ Weekly check-in routine
☐ Monthly dashboard

The most important tool I am missing is: *(choose one)*

☐ Budget template
☐ Debt tracker
☐ Savings tracker
☐ Separate bank accounts
☐ Automation
☐ Calendar reminders

☐ Weekly check-in routine
☐ Monthly dashboard

Financial tools can be simple: a budget template, a debt tracker, separate accounts for bills and spending, calendar reminders, automated transfers, and weekly check-ins. Tools remove friction. For example, separating money into "buckets" (Bills, Spending, Saving, Debt) reduces overspending because you can physically see limits. Automation reduces missed payments and keeps savings growing. A good tool doesn't just track money—it directs money.

Exercise: Build Your Financial Tool Stack

The tool I need for budgeting is: ________________________

The tool I need for debt tracking is: _____________________

The tool I need for saving is: ___________________________

The tool I need for planning is: _________________________

The first tool I will set up or improve is: ________________

Systems also create visibility. You need a way to see your progress clearly so you stay encouraged. That includes a debt payoff tracker, a savings milestone chart, and a monthly dashboard that shows your net worth improving over time. Visibility creates motivation because it gives your brain evidence. Evidence creates confidence. Confidence fuels discipline. That's a winning loop.

Exercise: Visibility Creates Motivation Dashboard

The progress I most need to see visually is:

- ☐ Debt balance
- ☐ Savings growth
- ☐ Net worth
- ☐ Credit score
- ☐ Spending control

My chosen tracking method is:

- ☐ Chart
- ☐ Spreadsheet
- ☐ App
- ☐ Printable tracker
- ☐ Dashboard

What visible proof would keep me encouraged right now?

____

Another essential system is a "financial review rhythm." Weekly: review accounts and spending. Monthly: plan your categories, pay down debt, update goals. Quarterly: check credit reports, evaluate insurance and subscriptions, adjust income strategies. This rhythm keeps you from drifting. It also prevents small issues from turning into emergencies.

Exercise: Financial Review Rhythm Builder

My weekly money review day is: ______________________

My monthly planning day is: ________________________

My quarterly review month is: _______________________

At my weekly review I will check: ______________________

At my monthly review I will update: ____________________

At my quarterly review I will evaluate: __________________

Scripture supports order and intentional planning without overwhelming you: *"The plans of the diligent lead surely to abundance."* (Proverbs 21:5). Diligence isn't doing everything—it's doing the right things consistently.

Finally, tools and systems protect your peace. Peace is not produced by hoping things work out. Peace is produced by knowing your money is organized, your plan is active, and your progress is measurable. When systems run, your stress goes down because you're no longer guessing—you're managing.

Exercise: Peace Through Structure Reflection

The part of money management that causes me the most stress is: ______________________________________

What system would reduce that stress? _________________

What would peace look like in my financial life? __________

Closing Reflection: Resources Turn Goals into Reality

The education resource I need is: ______________________

The mentor or support I need is: ______________________

The tool or system I need is: ___________________________

The first external resource I will activate is: _______________

The date I will begin is: ___________________

Internal resources fuel you from the inside. External resources support you from the outside. When you combine both, your success becomes less dependent on your mood and more dependent on your structure. And that's when financial freedom stops being a dream and starts becoming your lifestyle.

You now have the full Financial Progression System framework: location, destination, route, mode of travel, and resources. The next step is simple—but powerful: implement. Not perfectly. Consistently. And if you're aligned with the Debt Eliminator pathway, your learning can now become your acceleration—because you'll have step-by-step training, community support, and a plan designed to move you toward debt freedom, credit strength, and retirement building with confidence.

You're not just informed now.
You're equipped.
And you're ready to move.

Chapter 21: Leveraging Technology

Technology is not the solution—technology is the amplifier. It strengthens whatever system you commit to.

If money has ever felt confusing, overwhelming, or hard to manage consistently, technology can become one of your greatest advantages. Not because apps are magical—but because they reduce friction. They help you see what you used to ignore, remember what you used to forget, and stay consistent when life gets busy. In the Financial Progression System, technology is a resource that turns discipline into a system that runs smoothly.

Exercise: Technology & Money Friction Audit

The parts of money management that feel hardest for me are:

The parts I often forget, avoid, or delay are:

If technology could remove one point of financial friction in my life, it would be:

This helps the reader connect tools to real pain points.

But here's the key: tools don't create transformation—**habits do**. Technology simply makes the right habits easier and the wrong habits harder.

Exercise: Habit First, Tool Second Reflection

The financial habit I most need to strengthen is:

☐ **Zero-Based Budgeting:** Giving every dollar a "job" (e.g., $100 to groceries, $50 to savings) so there is $0 left over at the end of the month.

☐ **The Emergency Buffer:** Keeping 3–6 months of living expenses in a high-yield savings account ($HYSA$).

☐ **Dollar-Cost Averaging:** Investing a fixed amount of money at regular intervals, regardless of whether the stock market is up or down.

☐ **Credit Monitoring:** Checking your credit report regularly to catch errors or identity theft early.

☐ **The "Pay Yourself First" Rule:** Automatically transferring a set amount to savings or investments the moment your paycheck hits, before paying any bills.

The tool that could support that habit is:

☐ A dedicated budgeting app
☐ A credit monitoring app
☐ Automatic Alerts

If I rely on the tool without building the habit, what could go wrong? ____

How will I make sure the tool supports discipline instead of replacing attention? ________________________________

This chapter will show you how to use budgeting tools, credit monitoring, and automation/alerts in a way that removes uncertainty, builds momentum, and creates a steady dopamine loop through visible progress.

Budgeting Tools

Budgeting tools are best understood as "financial dashboards." A dashboard doesn't drive the car—it shows you what's happening so you can drive wisely. The right budgeting tool helps you understand cash flow, categorize spending, track progress toward goals, and reduce the stress of guessing where your money went. This alone is powerful because uncertainty is one of the biggest triggers of financial anxiety.

There are two main types of budgeting tools: **manual-entry tools** and **linked-account tools**. Manual tools require you to enter spending intentionally, which increases awareness fast and is excellent for people rebuilding discipline. Linked tools automatically pull transactions from your bank accounts and credit cards, which increases convenience and helps you track quickly. Neither is "better" universally—the best one is the one you will actually use weekly without quitting.

Exercise: Budgeting Tool Match Finder

Manual-entry may fit me if:	**Linked-account tools may fit me if:**
I need more awareness	I need convenience
I overspend without thinking	I am already somewhat organized
I want to slow down spending	I want faster tracking
I learn best by entering numbers myself	I prefer dashboards and automatic syncing

Which tool style fits my current season best?

☐ Manual ☐ Linked

Why? ______________________________________

A smart approach is to start simple and level up. If budgeting has been difficult in the past, you don't need 25 categories. You need clarity. Start with a small set of categories: housing, utilities, groceries, transportation, debt, savings, and discretionary. Once you can consistently track these, you can expand into more detail. The goal is not complexity—the goal is control.

Exercise: Simple Category Starter Budget

My starting budget categories are:

Housing:	$
Utilities:	$
Groceries:	$
Transportation:	$
Debt:	$

Savings:	$
Discretionary:	$
Total	$

Which one category do I most need technology to help me track better? ____________________

Budgeting tools also become powerful when you connect them to goals. Instead of only tracking spending, you track wins: "debt reduced this month," "savings increased," "credit utilization lowered," "subscriptions canceled," "cash flow improved." When you see these wins in a dashboard, it becomes encouraging. Your brain begins to associate budgeting with progress instead of restriction.

This month I want my budgeting dashboard to track:

Debt reduced by: $_________

Savings increased by: $_________

Subscriptions canceled: _________

Cash flow improved by: $_________

Credit utilization lowered to: _________%

Which number would encourage me the most to see improve this month? ____________________

And scripture supports this idea of intentional planning without pressure: *"The plans of the diligent lead surely to abundance."* (Proverbs 21:5). Budgeting tools help you plan like the diligent—so abundance becomes predictable.

Credit Monitoring

Credit monitoring is your early-warning system.

Exercise: Credit Monitoring Awareness Check

How often do I currently check my credit?

☐ Weekly ☐ Monthly ☐ Rarely ☐ Never

Do I currently know:

My approximate credit score?	☐ Yes ☐ No
Whether all accounts are accurate?	☐ Yes ☐ No
Whether there are hard inquiries I recognize?	☐ Yes ☐ No
Whether any collections appear?	☐ Yes ☐ No

The biggest surprise I would want to avoid is: ____________

Most people don't check credit until something goes wrong—denial for a loan, a surprise collection, or an unexpected score drop. That's like only checking your car engine after it breaks down. Credit monitoring helps you stay aware before problems become emergencies, and awareness gives you control.

There are three major benefits to credit monitoring. First, it helps you track progress—so when your score rises, you can see it and stay motivated. Second, it helps you identify errors—like accounts that aren't yours, incorrect late payments, outdated balances, or duplicate collections. Third, it helps protect against identity theft by alerting you when new accounts, inquiries, or unusual activity appears.

To eliminate uncertainty, understand this clearly: credit monitoring does not "fix" your credit by itself. It shows you what's happening so you can take action. Your score improves through consistent behaviors: on-time payments, lower utilization, fewer new inquiries, and resolving negatives when possible. Monitoring simply makes those changes visible and keeps you from being surprised.

Exercise: Credit Monitoring Action Plan

The credit behaviors I am currently working on are:

- ☐ On-time payments
- ☐ Lower utilization
- ☐ Fewer inquiries
- ☐ Disputing errors
- ☐ Paying collections
- ☐ Other

My credit check-in rhythm will be:

- ☐ Weekly
- ☐ Biweekly
- ☐ Monthly

If I see an error, my first response will be: ________________

If I see score improvement, I will use that as proof that:

____

Credit monitoring also helps you think strategically. If you're planning major moves—buying a car, applying for a mortgage, getting business funding—monitoring lets you watch your utilization and timing. You can reduce balances before applying, avoid unnecessary inquiries, and make sure your reports are accurate. That turns credit from something mysterious into something manageable.

Exercise: Major Move Credit Readiness Checklist

Before applying for a car, mortgage, or business funding, I will:

- ☐ Check my score
- ☐ Review utilization
- ☐ Verify report accuracy
- ☐ Avoid unnecessary inquiries
- ☐ Reduce balances if possible

My next major financial move is: ____________________

The date I want to be ready by is: ______________________

This turns credit monitoring into strategic preparation.

Scripture aligns with the wisdom of paying attention and guarding your life: *"The prudent see danger and take refuge."* (Proverbs 22:3). Monitoring is modern prudence. It's you choosing to see what's happening and respond early—so you don't pay unnecessary interest, fees, or higher premiums because you didn't know what was on your report.

Automation and Alerts

Automation is the technology version of discipline. It's one decision you make now that protects you repeatedly later.

When you automate key parts of your financial plan, you remove the need for perfect memory and constant motivation. That is essential because even the most disciplined people get tired, distracted, or overwhelmed at times.

Exercise: Automation Priority Builder

The first things I should automate are:

Options:

Minimum debt payments
Bills
Emergency fund transfer
Retirement contribution
Opportunity fund transfer

1. ______________________________
2. ______________________________
3. ______________________________

The one automation I will set up first is:

- ☐ Minimum debt payments
- ☐ Bills
- ☐ Emergency fund transfer
- ☐ Retirement contribution
- ☐ Opportunity fund transfer

The date I will set it up is: ______________________

The first priority for automation is **bill payments**, especially minimum debt payments. Late payments destroy credit and create fees that drain cash flow. Auto pay protects you from unnecessary damage. The second priority is **savings automation**—setting up automatic transfers into emergency, opportunity, and retirement accounts. This ensures you pay yourself first instead of hoping something is left at the end of the month.

Alerts are your backup system. Even if you automate, alerts help you stay aware. Set alerts for low balances, large transactions, upcoming due dates, and credit card utilization thresholds. Alerts reduce financial blind spots. They help you catch a leak quickly, stop fraud quickly, and avoid overdrafts or missed payments. Think of alerts as your financial "check engine light"—not scary, just informative.

Exercise: Financial Alerts Setup Plan

I need alerts for:

Low balance:	☐ Yes ☐ No
Large purchase:	☐ Yes ☐ No
Upcoming due date:	☐ Yes ☐ No
Credit utilization threshold:	☐ Yes ☐ No
New inquiry or account:	☐ Yes ☐ No

The alert that would protect me most right now is:

☐ Low balance
☐ Large purchase
☐ Upcoming due date
☐ Credit utilization threshold
☐ New inquiry or account

Why? ____

Automation and alerts also support emotional regulation. When money is stressful, people avoid it. But when systems are running, the fear decreases because the plan is working even when you're busy. This creates peace. Your brain starts trusting the system. And when you trust the system, you stop making panic decisions.

Scripture supports this principle of order and consistency: *"Let all things be done decently and in order."* (1 Corinthians 14:40). Automation is order. Alerts are awareness. Together, they create stability and reduce stress. And when stress decreases, consistency increases—which is what accelerates wealth.

Now that you understand how to leverage technology for budgeting, credit monitoring, and automation, the next chapter will focus on something just as powerful as tools: **people**. Because even the best system grows faster when you are surrounded by accountability, encouragement, and wise support.

Technology helps you track and automate. Community helps you stay strong and consistent.

Chapter 22: Community & Accountability

Financial freedom is easier when you stop trying to win alone.

Money is personal—but it was never meant to be private to the point of isolation. Many people stay stuck financially not because they lack intelligence or desire, but because they're carrying the journey alone. When you're alone, discouragement has more room to speak. Temptation has fewer obstacles. Confusion has no one to challenge it. And setbacks feel heavier because there's no external voice reminding you that you can reroute and keep going.

This chapter is about building the kind of support system that turns financial growth into something sustainable. Community doesn't replace discipline—it strengthens it. Accountability doesn't control you—it accelerates you. And when you have both, you'll notice something powerful: progress feels lighter, wins feel bigger, and the journey feels possible again.

Exercise: Isolation Inventory

In my financial life, the areas where I feel most alone are:

____

The money decisions I tend to carry by myself are:

____

The cost of that isolation has been:

- ☐ Confusion
- ☐ Delay
- ☐ Shame
- ☐ Fear
- ☐ Poor decisions
- ☐ Inconsistency
- ☐ Other

If I had stronger support, what would likely improve first?

____

Why Isolation Delays Wealth

Isolation delays wealth because isolation delays learning. When you have no one to process decisions with, you're more likely to make slow, uninformed, or emotional choices. You might delay budgeting, ignore credit reports, or avoid dealing with debt because you don't feel supported. Isolation makes simple decisions feel heavy, and heavy decisions usually get postponed.

Exercise: Why Isolation Delays Me Reflection

A financial decision I have been postponing is: ____________

Why have I been avoiding it? ____________________

Would support make this decision easier? ☐ Yes ☐ No

What kind of support would help most? ________________

Isolation also delays wealth because it increases shame. Many people are not hiding their finances because they're reckless—they're hiding because they're embarrassed. And shame thrives in secrecy.

Exercise: Shame Breaker Worksheet

The part of my financial life I feel most embarrassed about is:

____

What story have I been telling myself about this struggle?

____

What would change if I brought this into a safe, wise, supportive conversation?

____

The longer money struggles stay hidden; the longer unhealthy patterns remain unchallenged. Isolation allows financial pain to become "normal," even when it's draining your life.

Another reason isolation delays wealth is because it creates a lack of exposure. Exposure matters. When you spend time around people who plan, save, invest, and build, your mind expands. You begin to see what's possible.

Exercise: Exposure Expands Possibility Audit

The people I spend the most time around financially tend to be:

- ☐ Stressed
- ☐ Stable
- ☐ Avoidant
- ☐ Intentional
- ☐ Mixed

What financial habits are normal in my current environment?

____

What kind of financial environment do I need more of?

____

You learn vocabulary, strategies, and habits that weren't modeled for you before. But when you're isolated, your "normal" becomes whatever you've experienced—and if what you've experienced is paycheck-to-paycheck living, debt cycles, and financial stress, it's easy to believe that's just how life is.

Isolation also reduces resilience. When life hits—an emergency, a job change, a major bill—people who are isolated are more likely to panic, borrow, or quit their plan because they don't have emotional reinforcement or wise counsel. Community doesn't remove problems, but it increases your ability to handle problems without falling apart. It strengthens your mindset when your circumstances feel unstable.

Scripture speaks to this principle without pressure: *"Two are better than one… if either of them falls down, one can help the other up."*

(Ecclesiastes 4:9–10). Financially, this is powerful. If you slip, community helps you rise.

Exercise: Who Helps Me Rise?

When I am discouraged financially, the people most likely to help me refocus are:

1. ____________________
2. ____________________
3. ____________________

Who in my life offers wisdom instead of shame?

____

Who in my life reinforces bad habits instead of healthy ones?

____

If you get discouraged, community helps you refocus. If you get tempted, community helps you remember your destination. Isolation delays wealth because it delays support. Support accelerates progress.

Accountability as Acceleration

Accountability is not someone policing you—it's someone partnering with you.

Exercise: Accountability Misconception Reframe

When I hear the word accountability, I usually think:

____

The reason I may resist accountability is:

____

A healthier definition of accountability for me is:

____

It is structured encouragement with measurable follow-through. Accountability accelerates wealth because it reduces inconsistency, and inconsistency is the primary enemy of financial progress. Most people don't fail because they don't know what to do—they fail because they don't stay consistent long enough for results to compound.

Exercise: Consistency Through Accountability Check

The habit I know I need to stay consistent with is:

____

What usually causes me to drift? ____________________

How could regular check-ins help me stay on course?

____

What result would improve fastest if I stayed accountable for 90 days? ____________________________________

Accountability works because it interrupts self-negotiation. When you're accountable, you're less likely to say, "I'll start next week," or "It's fine, I'll catch up later." Accountability helps you take action in the moment. It turns intentions into appointments. It turns goals into reporting. And reporting creates momentum because you're not just planning—you're producing results you can share.

Another reason accountability accelerates wealth is because it turns progress into a scoreboard. When you check in weekly or monthly, you measure wins: debt reduced, savings increased, credit utilization lowered, spending under control. Your brain loves measurable wins. Wins create dopamine. Dopamine creates motivation. Motivation makes you consistent. And consistency compounds into freedom. Accountability creates more wins because it keeps you engaged with the process.

Exercise: My Financial Scoreboard

At each accountability check-in, I want to report on:

Debt reduced by: $________

Savings increased by: $________

Bills paid on time: ☐ Yes ☐ No

Credit utilization lowered to: ________

Spending plan followed: ☐ Yes ☐ No

My three most important progress indicators are:

1. ______________________________
2. ______________________________
3. ______________________________

Accountability also helps you course-correct faster. When you're alone, you might hide from your numbers for weeks after a setback. But accountability creates a quicker pivot: "Okay, what happened? What do we adjust? What's the next best step?" This is the GPS mindset in real time—reroute without restarting. A good accountability partner doesn't shame you for detours; they help you find the fastest way back to the route.

Exercise: Reroute Conversation Template

When I have a setback, my accountability conversation should answer:

What happened? ______________________________

What changed? ______________________________

What do I need to adjust? ____________________

What is my next best step? ___________________

What support do I need this week? ____________

____

Scripture captures this principle of sharpening and growth: *"As iron sharpens iron, so one person sharpens another."* (Proverbs 27:17). Accountability sharpens you. Not by criticism, but by clarity.

Exercise: Accountability Partner Profile

A good accountability partner for me should be:

- ☐ Trustworthy
- ☐ Encouraging
- ☐ Honest
- ☐ Consistent
- ☐ Non-shaming
- ☐ Goal-oriented

The person who may fit this role is: ____________________

If I do not have a person yet, the kind of group or program I need is: ____

This helps you stay committed to the version of you that you said you wanted to become. And when you stay committed long enough, you become that person naturally.

How to Build Community & Accountability Practically?

To eliminate uncertainty, here are practical forms accountability can take—without requiring perfection or big groups.

Exercise: Build Your Accountability Rhythm

My accountability structure will be:

- ☐ Money partner
- ☐ Spouse check-in
- ☐ Mentor
- ☐ Small group
- ☐ Coaching program
- ☐ Other ________________________

How often we will meet:

- ☐ Weekly
- ☐ Biweekly
- ☐ Monthly

What we will cover each time:

One win: __________________________________

One challenge: ______________________________

One next step: ______________________________

My first check-in date is: ___________________

You can have a "money partner" (a trusted friend or spouse) with a weekly 20-minute check-in. You can join a financial coaching program or learning community that provides structure and milestones. You can have a mentor who reviews your progress monthly. Or you can build a small group where everyone shares one win, one challenge, and one next step each week.

The key is simple: accountability must be consistent, measurable, and encouraging. It must focus on progress, not punishment.

Exercise: Encouragement-Not-Punishment Standard

My accountability should help me feel:

☐Encouraged
☐ Clear
☐ Focused
☐ Honest
☐ Supported

It should not make me feel:

☐ Ashamed
☐ Compared
☐ Controlled
☐ Defeated
☐ Hidden

If accountability becomes unhealthy, I will know because:

____

And it must be aligned with your destination. If you're building debt freedom and wealth, you need accountability that reinforces discipline, not accountability that pressures you into comparison or shame.

End-of-Chapter Community & Accountability Commitment

I am no longer trying to build financial freedom alone.

The support I need most right now is: ___________________

My accountability structure will be: _____________________

The person or program I will reach out to is: ____________

____

My first check-in or support step will happen on: ________

____

Now that you understand why isolation delays wealth and why accountability accelerates it, the next chapter will take you into a powerful next level: building relationships that expand your opportunities—partnerships, networks, and circles that increase your exposure, knowledge, and access.

You were never meant to build alone.
Now you're learning how to build with support—and speed.

PART VII — ESTIMATED TIME OF ARRIVAL (ETA)

Progress feels faster when time becomes predictable.

One of the most emotionally draining parts of financial struggle is not just the bills—it's the uncertainty. When you don't know how long you'll be in debt, how long you'll feel stressed, or how long it will take to breathe again, the mind starts to spiral. That's why ETA is powerful. A GPS doesn't just tell you where you're going—it tells you **when you're expected to arrive**.

This part of the Financial Progression System is designed to give you predictability. Not fantasy. Not vague hope. Real timelines based on your numbers and your strategy. When time becomes predictable, discipline becomes easier because your brain can see the finish line. And when you can see the finish line, you stop quitting in the middle.

Chapter 23: Building Timelines for Debt Freedom

9–24 Month Payoff Strategies

Debt freedom within 9–24 months is not reserved for high earners. It's reserved for people who combine clarity, structure, and consistent execution. The timeline depends on three things: your total debt, your cash flow margin, and your willingness to either reduce expenses, increase income, or both. The strategy is not magic—it's focused intensity for a defined season.

Exercise: My Debt Freedom ETA Calculator

My total debt balance is: $________

The monthly amount I can apply toward debt is: $________

Estimated payoff months = Total Debt ÷ Monthly Debt Payment

My estimated debt-free timeline is: ________ months

Does this timeline feel realistic, aggressive, or too loose for me?

____

A **9-month payoff strategy** is the "sprint." It requires aggressive focus and usually works best for people with moderate consumer debt or strong cash flow potential. The formula is simple: identify your total payoff target, divide it by 9, then build a plan to consistently hit that monthly number. This often includes cutting leaks aggressively, temporarily reducing lifestyle spending, using side income, and applying every extra dollar to debt. The key is that it's temporary. You're not sacrificing forever—you're locking in for a season to buy back years of freedom.

Exercise: 9-Month Sprint Test

If I wanted to be debt-free in 9 months, I would need to pay:

$________ per month

To make that happen, I would need to:

Cut expenses by: $________
Increase income by: $________
Redirect extra money from: ____________________

Is a 9-month sprint possible for me right now?

☐ Yes ☐ No ☐ Maybe with changes

A **12-month payoff strategy** is the "one-year mission." This is one of the most psychologically powerful timelines because it's long enough to be realistic and short enough to feel urgent. Many people can commit to a one-year push because they can picture life being different by this time next year. It often includes a combination of expense discipline, structured debt method (snowball/avalanche), and a modest income boost. It's also the timeline that fits beautifully with your Debt Eliminator / Debt Conqueror ecosystem because it turns learning into a measurable transformation window.

Exercise: One-Year Mission Builder

If I wanted to be debt-free in 12 months, I would need to pay:

$________ per month

My 12-month mission includes:

Main debt strategy: ____________________
Expense reduction goal: $________
Income increase goal: $________
Monthly debt target: $________

What would be being debt-free by this time next year make possible in my life?

____

A **18–24 month payoff strategy** is the "marathon with momentum." This is ideal for people with larger balances, more responsibilities, or less immediate cash flow. The benefit of this route is sustainability. You can still make major progress without feeling financially suffocated. You build the plan around consistent payments, automation, milestone celebrations, and periodic income increases. The danger is complacency—so the route must include tracking and mini-deadlines to maintain urgency without pressure.

Exercise: 18–24 Month Sustainable Route Planner

If I choose an 18-month route, I need to pay: $__________ per month

If I choose a 24-month route, I need to pay: $__________ per month

The route that feels most sustainable for me is: __________

Why? ______________________________________

To stay urgent without pressure, I will create check-in points every:

☐30 days ☐ 60 days ☐ 90 days

Scripture supports this idea of focused effort with a clear finish: *"Write the vision and make it plain…"* (Habakkuk 2:2). Making it plain includes putting dates to it. A payoff timeline written down turns debt from an emotional cloud into a scheduled project. And a scheduled project is far easier to execute than an undefined burden.

Exercise: My Chosen Debt Freedom Date

My chosen debt-free date is: ________________

My chosen payoff timeline is: ________ months

The reason I am choosing this date is: ________________

____

My monthly payment target is: $________

Momentum-Based Planning

Momentum-based planning is the difference between a plan you follow and a plan you abandon. Most people don't quit because the math is hard—they quit because the journey feels emotionally unrewarding. Momentum-based planning ensures you experience regular wins so your brain stays engaged. Momentum begins with **early wins**.

Exercise: Momentum Starter Win

The fastest early win I can create is: ______________

The debt I can pay off first is: __________________

The balance of that debt is: $____________

The date I want it gone by is: __________________

How will this win help me believe again?

____

That's why many people thrive with the snowball method—because paying off one small debt quickly creates psychological energy. That energy is not childish—it's strategic. When you see something disappear, you believe again. Belief is fuel. Fuel produces consistency. Consistency produces bigger wins. And that cycle becomes addictive in a healthy way.

Momentum-based planning also uses **milestones** to measure progress beyond the final payoff. Instead of only celebrating "debt-free day," you celebrate 10% down, 25% down, first account paid off, utilization under 50%, then under 30%, savings hitting $500, then $1,000. These milestones create dopamine throughout the journey, which makes the journey feel faster because it's filled with victories instead of waiting.

Exercise: Milestones, Not Just the Finish Line

My debt payoff milestones are:

10% paid off by: ___________________

25% paid off by: ___________________

50% paid off by: ___________________

First account paid off by: ___________________

Debt-free date: ___________________

Which milestone will motivate me the most when I hit it?

____

Another key is **momentum stacking**—using each win to unlock the next level. For example, once a debt is paid off, you don't "free up money to spend." You roll that payment into the next debt (snowball). Or once your credit score rises, you refinance a high-interest loan, which reduces payments, which increases cash flow, which speeds payoff. Momentum stacking is how the journey accelerates over time instead of staying the same speed.

Exercise: Momentum Stacking Plan

When this debt is paid off, I will roll $________ into the next debt.

When my credit improves, I may: ________________

When my income increases, I will assign the extra $________ to: ____________________

When one bill disappears, I will redirect it toward:

____

Scripture frames momentum through steadfast progress: *"The path of the righteous is like the morning sun, shining ever brighter till the full light of day."* (Proverbs 4:18). That "brighter" path is momentum. It starts dim, then grows. The more you move, the easier moving becomes. The more you win, the more you expect to win.

Exercise: My Brighter Path Reflection

In the beginning, my path may feel dim because:

____

What signs will show me that it is getting brighter?

____

What would make me feel momentum in the next 30 days?

____

Exercise: Debt Freedom Timeline Summary Sheet

My debt-free date is: ____________________

My monthly payment target is: $________

My chosen timeline is: ☐ 9 ☐ 12 ☐ 18 ☐ 24 months

My first early win is: ____________________

My next milestone is: ____________________

The income/expense move that supports this timeline is: ____________________

Now that you know how to build a debt freedom ETA and use momentum-based planning, the next chapter will focus on protecting your timeline from the number one enemy of progress: **unexpected interruptions and lifestyle drift.**

End-of-Chapter Commitment Statement

Debt freedom is no longer a vague desire for me. It is now a project with a date.

My date is: ____________________

My reason is: ________________________________

My first payment move is: ____________________

My next step this week is: ____________________

In the next chapter, we'll build a "timeline protection plan" that includes buffers, emergency strategy, and systems that keep you on course even when life gets loud.

Your finish line is no longer a mystery. Now it's a date you can pursue—with confidence.

Chapter 24: Scheduling Wealth

Wealth becomes predictable when your finances have appointments, not intentions.

Most people don't fail financially because they don't care. They fail because money is managed in the leftover spaces of life—when there's time, when there's energy, when there's no stress. But life rarely gives you perfect conditions. That's why wealthy outcomes are rarely built by random bursts of motivation. They're built by **scheduled rhythm**.

Scheduling wealth means you treat your financial life like something that deserves structure—just like work meetings, doctor appointments, and important deadlines. When money has a schedule, it stops feeling like chaos. It becomes a system. And when it becomes a system, your progress speeds up because you eliminate the gaps where drift, leaks, and avoidance usually grow.

Exercise: Wealth Scheduling Reality Check

Right now, I usually deal with money:

☐ Only when there is a problem
☐ Randomly
☐ Weekly
☐ Monthly
☐ Other

The part of my financial life that feels most unscheduled is:

____

When money is left to "when I have time," what usually happens?

____

If I gave my finances a real schedule, the area that would improve first is: ________________________________

Weekly Money Meetings

A weekly money meeting is the simplest habit that produces the most stability. It doesn't need to be long, complicated, or stressful. Fifteen to thirty minutes once a week can change your entire financial life because it keeps you aware and proactive.

Exercise: Weekly Money Meeting Appointment Setter

My weekly money meeting day will be: __________________

My weekly money meeting time will be: __________________

My meeting length will be: ☐ 15 ☐ 20 ☐ 30 minutes

My meeting location will be at: ________________________

If I share money with someone, who will attend with me?

____

What would make this meeting easy enough to keep every week?

___

Weekly meetings prevent "surprises," and most financial anxiety comes from surprise. The purpose of the weekly meeting is not to create a full budget from scratch. The purpose is to check your route:

Exercise: Weekly Money Meeting Agenda

When you answer these questions weekly, money stops being a mystery. And when money isn't a mystery, it stops controlling your emotions.

At each weekly money meeting I will review:

What came in this week: ___

What went out this week: ___

Bills coming next: ___

Any overspending category: ___

Any money leak or surprise: ___

One win from this week: ___

One adjustment for next week: ___

This makes weekly oversight simple and sustainable.

Weekly meetings also create momentum. You get to track wins in real time: "We stayed under groceries." "We didn't eat out this week." "We made an extra debt payment." "Savings moved automatically." These wins are not small—they are the building blocks of financial confidence.

Exercise: Weekly Wins Tracker

This week I won by:

- ☐ Staying under budget in one category
- ☐ Avoiding an impulse purchase
- ☐ Making an extra debt payment
- ☐ Moving money to savings
- ☐ Reviewing my accounts
- ☐ Catching a problem early

My biggest financial win this week was: ____________________

Your brain responds to visible progress. It begins to crave the feeling of completion and control. If you're married or managing money with a partner, weekly meetings become a relationship stabilizer too. They reduce assumptions and resentment. Instead of arguing after the money is gone, you agree before it's spent. You build teamwork instead of tension.

Exercise: Money Meeting Relationship Builder

If I manage money with a partner, our weekly meeting will focus on:

☐ Agreement before spending
☐ Shared goals
☐ Upcoming expenses
☐ One win and one challenge

The conversation I most need us to have is: ____________

____

Even if you're doing it solo, the meeting creates self-trust—because you're showing up for your future consistently.

The self-trust I want to build through this meeting is:

____

Scripture supports the wisdom of consistent oversight: *"Be sure you know the condition of your flocks, give careful attention to your herds."* (Proverbs 27:23). In modern terms, your accounts and bills are your "flocks." Attention prevents loss. Weekly money meetings are a form of stewardship that keeps you protected.

Monthly Reviews

Monthly reviews are where you stop reacting and start improving. Weekly meetings keep you on track; monthly reviews make you better. A monthly review is your chance to zoom out and ask: What worked? What didn't? What changed? What needs adjustment?

Exercise: Monthly Review Scorecard

This is where you refine your financial system like a leader—calmly, intelligently, and without shame.

This month:

Total income	$
Total expenses	$
Debt reduced by	$
Savings increased by	$
Credit utilization now	%

What worked well this month? ___________________________

What didn't work well this month? _______________________

What must change next month? ___________________________

A strong monthly review includes reviewing income totals, expenses by category, debt balances, savings progress, and credit utilization. You're not doing this to criticize yourself. You're doing it to identify patterns. Patterns reveal where you're leaking, where you're strong, and where you need a new strategy. If you notice that weekends cause overspending, you don't just "try harder"—you build a weekend plan. If groceries are always over, you adjust the category or change shopping strategy.

Exercise: Pattern Spotting Worksheet

The category I most often overspend in is: ______________

The day or time I am most vulnerable is: ________________

The emotional trigger that affects spending most is: _______

____

The financial habit I did well with this month is: __________

____

Monthly reviews also include upcoming planning. What expenses are coming next month? Are there birthdays, school fees, travel, car maintenance, or seasonal bills? When you plan monthly, you stop being ambushed by predictable expenses.

Exercise: Next Month Planning Sheet

Next month I need to prepare for:

- ☐ Birthdays
- ☐ Travel
- ☐ Maintenance
- ☐ School fees
- ☐ Insurance
- ☐ Holidays
- ☐ Other

Upcoming planned expenses:

Expense	Amount

To prepare, I will set aside: $________

The category I need to adjust next month is: ______________

This reduces stress dramatically. One of the biggest upgrades in adulthood is realizing most "emergencies" aren't emergencies—they're expenses you didn't prepare for.

Monthly reviews create a dopamine loop because you can see the scoreboard. Debt shrinking, savings growing, spending improving, confidence rising—these are measurable results. The monthly review is where you celebrate those wins and set the next month's targets. That celebration matters. Celebration is not distraction—it's reinforcement. It tells your brain, "This discipline is working."

Exercise: Monthly Celebration and Target Reset

This month I am proud of:

____

The best result I created this month was:

____

The one target I want to hit next month is:

____

The one habit I want to strengthen next month is:

____

Scripture supports this idea of review and adjustment: *"Let us examine our ways and test them…"* (Lamentations 3:40). Examination is not condemnation—it's correction. Monthly reviews help you correct course without quitting, and they keep your ETA realistic and achievable.

Annual Financial Audits

An annual financial audit is where you step into full financial leadership. It's your once-a-year deep review to ensure your entire financial structure is aligned with your goals and your life season. While weekly and monthly check-ins maintain the system, the annual audit upgrades it.

Exercise: Annual Financial Audit Checklist

Once each year I will review:

- ☐ Net worth
- ☐ Total debt reduction
- ☐ Savings growth
- ☐ Retirement contributions
- ☐ Credit reports
- ☐ Insurance coverage
- ☐ Beneficiaries
- ☐ Fees and subscriptions
- ☐ Long-term goals
- ☐ Estate documents

My annual audit month will be: ___________________

☐ January	☐ February	☐ March
☐ April	☐ May	☐ June
☐ July	☐ August	☐ September
☐ October	☐ November	☐ December

An annual audit includes reviewing your net worth, total debt reduction for the year, savings growth, retirement contributions, credit reports, insurance coverage, and major financial documents. You're asking bigger questions: Are we protected properly? Are we insured adequately? Are we underinsured? Are we investing enough? Are we paying unnecessary fees? Are we still aligned with our financial freedom destination? This is where you catch silent leaks that can cost thousands over time.

Annual audits also include "life change recalibration." If you got married, had a child, changed jobs, moved, started a business, or experienced a major medical event, your financial strategy must adjust. Your budget should change. Your insurance needs may change. Your savings targets may change. Your retirement plan may change. Annual audits make sure your plan matches your reality—not your past.

Exercise: Life Change Recalibration Sheet

Major changes in my life this year:

☐ Marriage	☐ Job change
☐ Child	☐ Business start
☐ Move	☐ Health event
☐ Other: ____________________________	

Because of this change, I may need to adjust:

- ☐ Budget
- ☐ Insurance
- ☐ Savings target
- ☐ Debt plan
- ☐ Retirement
- ☐ Estate documents

The most urgent adjustment I need to make is: ___________

This is also the best time to address legacy-focused tasks: wills, beneficiaries, estate planning, and long-term goals. Many people avoid these topics because they feel heavy, but in reality, they are acts of love and wisdom. Getting your documents in order protects your family, reduces future confusion, and reflects true stewardship.

Exercise: Legacy and Protection Review

Do I currently have:

A will?	☐ Yes ☐ No
Updated beneficiaries?	☐ Yes ☐ No
Adequate insurance?	☐ Yes ☐ No
Emergency documents organized?	☐ Yes ☐ No
A legacy plan in progress?	☐ Yes ☐ No

The first protective step I need to take is: _______________

____

Scripture honors this kind of preparation and responsibility: *"A good man leaves an inheritance to his children's children…"* (Proverbs 13:22). An inheritance is not only money—it's structure, protection, and planning. Annual audits help you build that structure so your family isn't left with chaos. And when you do this yearly, you start living like someone who expects to win long-term.

Exercise: My Wealth Rhythm Calendar

My weekly money meeting is: ____________________

My monthly review date is: ____________________

My annual financial audit month is: ________________

My non-negotiable wealth appointments are:

1. ____
2. ____
3. ____

End-of-Chapter Scheduling Commitment

I will no longer leave my finances to leftover time.

My first weekly money meeting will happen on: ___________

My next monthly review will happen on: _________________

My annual audit month will be: ____________________

The reason this schedule matters to my future is: __________

Now that you understand how to schedule wealth through weekly meetings, monthly reviews, and annual audits, the next chapter will focus on accelerating your timeline through one of the most powerful financial moves available: increasing income intentionally and strategically—without burning out.

You don't need more motivation.
You need a schedule that makes wealth inevitable.

PART VIII — YOU HAVE ARRIVED (AND WHAT'S NEXT)

Arrival is not the end—it's the launch point.

Debt freedom is one of the most powerful milestones a person can reach—not just financially, but emotionally. When the payments stop, the pressure lifts. When the balances hit zero, your mind gets quieter. When you realize your money is finally yours again, something changes inside you: you stop surviving and start building.

But here's the truth most people don't plan for: arriving at debt freedom is not automatic prosperity. It's a new season that requires new wisdom. Without a plan, the same cash flow that once paid debt will quietly get absorbed into spending, upgrades, and "deserved" conveniences. That's why this chapter exists—to make sure your arrival becomes a launch point into wealth, not a return trip back to bondage.

Chapter 25: Life After Debt

Redirecting Freed Cash Flow

When debt is gone, your cash flow expands. That expanded cash flow is a powerful resource—but it is also a temptation. Most people feel an emotional rush after becoming debt free, and rightfully so. The danger is using that rush to make permanent lifestyle commitments that consume the very margin you just fought to create. The key is to celebrate your freedom without spending your freedom away.

Exercise: Freed Cash Flow Discovery

The total monthly amount I was paying toward debt was:

$________

Now that debt is gone, my monthly freed cash flow is:

$________

If I do nothing intentional with this money, it will most likely go toward:

____

The first reason this freed cash flow matters is:

____

The smartest move after debt is to give your freed cash flow a clear assignment. Money without an assignment will find one—usually through impulse or convenience. In FPS, your freed cash flow should be redirected into three priority areas: **safety, growth, and legacy**.

Exercise: Safety, Growth, Legacy Allocation Plan

My freed cash flow will now be assigned to:

Safety: $___________
Growth: $___________
Legacy: $___________

Safety will include: ______________________________

Growth will include: ______________________________

Legacy will include: ______________________________

Which of these three needs the most attention in my life right now?

☐ Safety
☐ Growth
☐ Legacy

This keeps post-debt money from becoming random money.

Safety includes strengthening emergency reserves and stabilizing monthly cash flow. Growth includes investing and income-building assets. Legacy includes giving, family stability, estate planning, and long-term impact.

First, build your safety layer. Even if you had a starter emergency fund while paying off debt, post-debt life is the season to expand it—typically toward 3–6 months of essential expenses, depending on job stability and household needs. This gives you protection from job changes, medical costs, unexpected repairs, and economic shifts. Safety is not fear—it's freedom insurance.

Exercise: Safety Layer Expansion Plan

My current emergency fund is: $_______________

My monthly essential expenses are: $____________

My target emergency fund is:

3 months = $___________

6 months = $___________

The amount I will redirect monthly toward this goal is: $___________

My target completion date is: ___________________

The bigger your buffer, the less you panic.

Second, redirect cash flow into wealth-building. This is where retirement contributions increase, investment accounts become consistent, and long-term goals move from "someday" to "scheduled." A simple strategy is to take a portion of what you were paying toward debt and automatically redirect it into investments. This keeps your lifestyle stable while your wealth grows quietly. If you were paying $600 toward debt monthly, imagine redirecting $400 into investing and $200 into savings—your life stays the same, but your future expands.

Exercise: Quiet Wealth Redirection Strategy

Of my freed cash flow, I will redirect:

To investing: $____________
To savings: $_____________
To other long-term goals: $____________

The account or system I will use is: ____________________

The date this redirect will begin is: ____________________

Scripture supports this principle of purposeful redirection: *"The wise store up choice food and olive oil…"* (Proverbs 21:20). Post-debt cash flow is "choice oil." If you consume it immediately, you return to scarcity. If you store and invest it intentionally, you create abundance. The dopamine in this season is watching your net worth rise—because you're no longer just eliminating negatives, you're building positives.

Exercise: Net Worth Rising Reflection

Before debt freedom, I was focused on: ________________

After debt freedom, I now want to focus on: ____________

The most exciting part of seeing my net worth rise will be:

____

Avoiding Lifestyle Inflation

Lifestyle inflation is the silent thief of arrival. It happens when your spending rises to match your new margin. The debt is gone, but your expenses increase—new car payment, upgraded subscriptions, bigger vacations, more eating out, higher housing costs. None of these things are inherently wrong. The danger is when upgrades become automatic and unplanned, turning your freed cash flow into a new form of financial pressure.

Exercise: Lifestyle Inflation Trigger Audit

The upgrades I feel most tempted to make right away are:

1. ______________________________
2. ______________________________
3. ______________________________

Why do these upgrades appeal to me right now?

____

Would these upgrades increase peace or increase pressure?

☐ Peace ☐ Pressure

Lifestyle inflation often begins emotionally. You tell yourself, "I deserve this." And maybe you do. But "deserve" without strategy can become a trap.

Exercise: "I Deserve This" Reframe

When I say "I deserve this," what I usually mean is:

____

A healthier way to reward myself would be:

____

A reward that honors both my freedom and my future is:

____

You didn't work hard to become debt free just to replace your old payments with new payments. Freedom isn't simply having more spending power—it's having more **options** and less stress. The goal is to keep your options open, not lock yourself into a new cycle of obligations.

To avoid lifestyle inflation, you need guardrails. One powerful guardrail is the **percentage rule**: as your margin grows, you decide in advance how much will go toward lifestyle upgrades versus wealth building. For example, you might choose: 70% of freed cash flow goes to savings/investing and 30% goes to lifestyle enjoyment. That allows celebration without sabotage. It keeps joy in the journey while protecting your future.

Exercise: Post-Debt Percentage Rule Builder

I will use the following post-debt cash flow rule:

Toward savings/investing: ________%

Toward lifestyle enjoyment: ________%

Toward giving/legacy: ____________%

Why this percentage split fits my current season:

____

This creates a guardrail before money gets reabsorbed into consumption.

Another guardrail is intentional "upgrade timing." Instead of upgrading immediately after debt freedom, give yourself a 90-day stability window. During that time, you redirect cash flow into savings and investments first, allowing your nervous system to recalibrate to peace. Then you upgrade intentionally, not emotionally. This is how you shift from impulsive spending to purposeful enjoyment. You learn to reward yourself without losing yourself.

Exercise: 90-Day Stability Window Plan

For the next 90 days after debt freedom, I will:

☐ Avoid major lifestyle upgrades
☐ Redirect freed cash flow into savings/investing
☐ Track how peace feels without debt
☐ Delay any major reward decision until the 90-day window ends

At the end of 90 days, I will reevaluate:

____

Scripture offers a steady reminder: *"Better is a little with righteousness than much gain with injustice."* (Proverbs 16:8). In modern terms: better is a stable life with peace than a flashy life with pressure. Lifestyle inflation is pressure disguised as reward. Real reward is the ability to breathe, save, invest, give, and build—without fear.

Exercise: Pressure vs. Peace Comparison

A flashy life with pressure looks like:

____

A stable life with peace looks like:

____

Which life am I actually trying to build?

____

Your Arrival Mindset: From Debt-Free to Wealth-Driven

The greatest shift after debt is not financial—it's identity. You move from "I'm trying to get out" to "I'm building up."

Exercise: Arrival Identity Shift

Before debt freedom, I saw myself as someone who was: ____

Now I want to see myself as someone who is: ____

The new financial identity I am stepping into is:

____

This turns debt freedom into a new beginning, not just an ending. That's a different mindset. It requires new goals, new milestones, and new excitement. Debt freedom is a finish line, but it is also the starting line for wealth creation. Now you start playing offense: assets, investments, retirement, property, business, and legacy.

Exercise: My Wealth-Driven Goals

Now that debt is behind me, my next top wealth goals are:

1. ____________________
2. ____________________
3. ____________________

The first wealth-building system I want to strengthen is: ____________________

The first asset I want to build or acquire is: ____________________

This gives the reader direction beyond debt.

The dopamine in this season is deeper than paying off balances. It's watching your net worth climb. It's seeing your accounts grow. It's realizing you can handle emergencies without panic. It's experiencing generosity without fear. It's looking back and knowing you became the kind of person who can win long-term.

Exercise: Post-Debt Launch Plan

My monthly freed cash flow is: $________

My first safety goal is: ____________________

My first growth goal is: ____________________

My first legacy goal is: ____________________

My lifestyle inflation guardrail is: ______________________

My 90-day post-debt commitment is: __________________

____

Now that you understand how to redirect freed cash flow and avoid lifestyle inflation, the next chapter will show you how to turn debt freedom into long-term wealth through systems like investing, retirement planning, and asset building—so your arrival becomes a launch into generational stability.

End-of-Chapter Legacy Statement

I did not get free just to become financially pressured again.

I got free so I could build.

What I will build now is: ____________________________

The first action I will take this week is: _________________

The legacy I want this new season to create is: ___________

____

You didn't just escape debt.
You earned the right to build a legacy.

Chapter 26: Building Wealth That Outlives You

True wealth is not measured by what you accumulate—but by what continues long after you're gone.

Debt freedom gives you breathing room. Wealth-building gives you options. But **legacy** gives your life financial meaning beyond yourself. This chapter marks the shift from personal success to generational impact. It's where you stop thinking only about your lifetime and start thinking about stewardship across lifetimes.

Exercise: Legacy Definition Statement

To me, wealth that outlives me means:

The people I most want my financial decisions to impact are:

If my life created lasting financial meaning, it would look like:

Building wealth that outlives you is not reserved for the ultra-rich. It is built through intentional systems, clear planning, and disciplined consistency. This chapter will remove confusion around retirement, insurance, estate planning, and generational thinking—so you can move forward confidently, knowing your financial house is built on rock, not sand.

Exercise: From Personal Success to Generational Stewardship Reflection

Until now, most of my financial thinking has been focused on:

☐ Survival	☐ Stability
☐ Debt freedom	☐ Comfort
☐ Growth	☐ Other

The next level of my financial thinking needs to focus on:

____

What does stewardship across lifetimes mean to me?

____

Retirement

Retirement is not about quitting work—it's about gaining **choice**. It's the ability to work because you want to, not because you have to. True retirement planning is about financial independence: having enough assets and income streams to support your lifestyle without relying on employment or others for survival.

Exercise: Retirement Readiness Snapshot

My current age is: ________

My desired retirement age is: ________

My current retirement contribution per month is: $________

Do I currently contribute consistently? ☐Yes ☐ No

What would financial independence mean for my life?

The biggest misconception about retirement is that it's "far away." In reality, retirement is built one contribution at a time. Consistent investing—especially when started early—creates compounding growth that does most of the heavy lifting. Time is your greatest ally. Even modest, regular contributions can grow into substantial security when discipline and time work together.

Exercise: One Contribution at a Time Plan

The amount I can begin or continue contributing monthly is:

$____________

The retirement account I am using or plan to use is:

____

The date I will automate or review this contribution is:

____

If my income increases, I will raise this contribution by:

$____________ or __________%

Another critical shift is understanding that retirement planning is not "extra money"—it's priority money. It should be automated, protected, and increased intentionally as income grows. Many people wait until they feel "comfortable" to invest for retirement, but comfort rarely arrives without preparation. You don't wait to feel secure to save—you save to become secure.

Exercise: Retirement Priority Reframe

The reason I have delayed retirement planning is:

____

What would change in my future if I took it seriously now?

____

One belief I need to adopt about retirement is:

____

Scripture supports this wisdom of preparation without fear: *"Go to the ant, you sluggard; consider its ways and be wise… it stores its provisions in summer."* (Proverbs 6:6–8). Retirement planning is modern-day storing in summer. It's not pessimism—it's foresight. And foresight creates peace.

The dopamine in retirement planning comes from watching independence take shape. Each contribution is proof that your future is being funded intentionally. You're no longer postponing security—you're building it.

Insurance

Insurance is not about expecting disaster—it's about protecting progress. You didn't work hard to eliminate debt and build wealth just to have it wiped out by one unexpected event. Insurance is the guardrail that keeps a single moment from becoming a financial collapse.

At its core, insurance transfers risk. Instead of one event destroying your savings, income, or family stability, insurance absorbs the impact. The most important forms of insurance include health, life, disability, auto, home, and umbrella coverage. Each serves a different role, but all exist for the same reason: **protection of legacy**.

Exercise: Protection Gap Audit

Do I currently have:

Health insurance?	☐ Yes ☐ No
Life insurance?	☐ Yes ☐ No
Disability insurance?	☐ Yes ☐ No
Auto insurance?	☐ Yes ☐ No
Home or renters insurance?	☐ Yes ☐ No
Umbrella coverage?	☐ Yes ☐ No

The greatest protection gap in my life right now is:

____

Life insurance, in particular, is misunderstood. It's not about death—it's about continuity. It ensures your family has income replacement, debt coverage, and stability if something happens to you. For many households, life insurance is the foundation of generational protection. It prevents grief from becoming financial chaos.

Exercise: Insurance as Legacy Protection Reflection

If something happened to me, the people most financially affected would be:

____

What would I want protected for them?

☐ Income	☐ Housing
☐ Debt payoff	☐ Education
☐ Stability	☐ Other _______________

The insurance protection I most need to review or strengthen is: ____________________________

Scripture affirms the responsibility of protection clearly: *"Anyone who does not provide for their relatives… has denied the faith."* (1 Timothy 5:8). Providing includes planning for what happens if you're not present. Insurance is not fear-driven—it's love-driven. It's stewardship with foresight.

When insurance is properly structured, it brings peace. You sleep better knowing that one incident won't undo years of discipline. Protection doesn't slow wealth—it preserves it.

Estate Planning

Estate planning is not about being wealthy—it's about being **responsible**. Without a plan, the courts decide what happens to your assets, your children, and your legacy. With a plan, *you* decide. Estate planning is one of the most loving financial acts you can perform because it removes confusion and conflict during emotionally difficult times.

A basic estate plan typically includes a will, power of attorney, healthcare directives, and updated beneficiaries. More advanced plans may include trusts, guardianship instructions, and charitable directives.

Exercise: Estate Planning Readiness Checklist

Do I currently have:

A will?	☐ Yes ☐ No
Power of attorney?	☐ Yes ☐ No
Healthcare directive?	☐ Yes ☐ No
Updated beneficiaries?	☐ Yes ☐ No
Trust (if needed)?	☐ Yes ☐ No
Guardianship instructions (if needed)?	☐ Yes ☐ No

The first estate planning document I need to complete or review is: ______________________________

These documents don't just distribute assets—they distribute clarity. They protect your intentions when you're no longer able to speak.

Exercise: If I Could No Longer Speak Plan

If I could no longer speak for myself, I would want these things to be clear:

1. ______________________________
2. ______________________________
3. ______________________________

The person I would trust to make decisions is:

____

The areas where my family would need the most clarity are:

____

Many people avoid estate planning because it feels uncomfortable or overwhelming. But avoidance is costly.

Exercise: Avoidance Cost Reflection

The reason I have avoided estate planning is:

____

What would be the cost of continuing to avoid it?

____

What peace would come from handling it now?

____

Families without estate plans often experience disputes, delays, and unnecessary legal expenses. A plan ensures your family spends time healing—not fighting paperwork and courtrooms.

Scripture emphasizes the importance of order and intentional inheritance: *"A good man leaves an inheritance to his children's children."* (Proverbs 13:22). An inheritance is not just money—it's structure, clarity, and protection. Estate planning is how you leave peace behind, not confusion.

The dopamine in estate planning comes from relief. Knowing things are handled. Knowing your wishes are clear. Knowing your family is protected. That peace is priceless.

Generational Thinking

Generational thinking is the highest level of financial maturity. It's when your decisions are no longer centered on consumption, but on **continuity**. You begin asking different questions: What systems am I leaving? What habits am I modeling? What knowledge am I passing down?

Exercise: Generational Thinking Audit

The financial habits I am currently modeling are:

____

The systems I want to leave behind are:

____

The knowledge I want the next generation to receive from me is: ____

Wealth is fragile when it's only transferred financially. It becomes powerful when it's transferred **educationally** and **culturally**. Teaching children how money works, how debt traps operate, how to save, invest, and give—this is how cycles are broken. This is how families stop starting over every generation.

Exercise: More Than Money Transfer Plan

Beyond money, I want to pass down:

- ☐ Discipline
- ☐ Stewardship
- ☐ Saving
- ☐ Investing
- ☐ Giving
- ☐ Business thinking
- ☐ Other ________________

The way I will begin teaching this is: ____________________

____

One conversation I need to have with the next generation is about: ____

Generational thinking also includes building assets that last: paid-off homes, businesses, investment accounts, insurance structures, and trusts. These assets reduce struggle for the next generation and increase opportunity. That doesn't create entitlement—it creates stability when paired with education and values.

Exercise: Asset Legacy Blueprint

The assets I want to build or preserve for the future are:

> *Examples: Paid-off home, Investment account, Retirement fund, Business, Insurance structure, Trust, College fund*

1. ______________________________
2. ______________________________
3. ______________________________

The first asset I will intentionally strengthen is: ___________

Scripture reflects this long view beautifully: *"We will tell the next generation the praiseworthy deeds of the Lord..."* (Psalm 78:4). Financial wisdom is part of that story. Passing down knowledge, discipline, and stewardship creates a lineage of confidence instead of confusion.

The dopamine of generational thinking is deeper than personal success. It's the satisfaction of knowing your discipline didn't stop with you. That your choices today will make life easier, stronger, and freer for people you may never meet—but who will live better because you planned.

Exercise: People I May Never Meet Reflection

The future people my decisions may impact include:

- ☐ Children
- ☐ Grandchildren
- ☐ Family members
- ☐ Community
- ☐ Ministry
- ☐ Others _______________

How could my discipline today make life easier for them?

____

Why does that matter to me?

____

Final Reflection: Legacy Is Built on Purpose

Exercise: Legacy on Purpose Summary Sheet

My retirement priority is: __________________

My insurance priority is: __________________

My estate planning priority is: __________________

My generational priority is: __________________

The first legacy-building action I will take is:

- ☐ Retirement
- ☐ Insurance
- ☐ Estate Planning
- ☐ Generational

The date I will begin is: __________________

Building wealth that outlives you is not about perfection—it's about intention. Retirement creates independence. Insurance protects progress. Estate planning preserves clarity. Generational thinking multiplies impact.

End-of-Chapter Legacy Declaration

I am not building only for my lifetime.

I am building for continuity, protection, and impact.

What I want to remain after me is: ____________________

What I will begin building now is: ____________________

The legacy I want my life to leave is: ____________________

You didn't just arrive at financial freedom.
You arrived at responsibility, influence, and legacy.

And now, you are no longer just passing through life financially.
You are building something that remains.

CONCLUSION: From Financial Survival to Financial Sovereignty

This is not the end of a book.
This is the end of confusion.

What you've just completed is more than a financial framework—it is a **personal transformation**. You didn't just learn how money works. You learned how *you* work with money. And that shift changes everything.

Financial sovereignty is not about perfection. It's about **position**. It's about no longer being reactive, no longer being driven by fear, pressure, or lack of knowledge. It's about moving with clarity, confidence, and command. You didn't just read pages—you installed a system. And systems change lives.

You Are No Longer Lost

There was a time when money felt overwhelming, confusing, and heavy. Bills arrived faster than peace. Decisions felt emotional instead of strategic. Progress felt accidental instead of predictable. You weren't irresponsible—you were **unmapped**. And when there's no map, every turn feels risky.

But now, you are no longer lost.

You know where you are financially because you faced it honestly. You separated net worth from self-worth. You confronted numbers without shame. You identified patterns without judgment. And in doing so, you reclaimed something powerful: **clarity**. Clarity removes fear. Clarity replaces anxiety with direction.

Being "lost" financially doesn't mean you lacked intelligence—it means you lacked a system. Now you have one. You understand your starting point, your destination, your route, your pace, and your resources. You no longer wander from paycheck to paycheck hoping things improve. You move forward knowing **why** and **how** they will.

Scripture reminds us, *"The steps of a good person are ordered."* (Psalm 37:23). Your steps are ordered now—not randomly, but intentionally. You are no longer guessing. You are navigating. And once you've experienced that level of clarity, you never accept confusion again.

You Now Move with Intention

Survival reacts. Sovereignty plans.

Before, money decisions may have been driven by urgency, emotion, or pressure. Now, they are driven by **intention**. You don't just spend—you assign. You don't just earn—you direct. You don't just hope—you schedule outcomes.

Intention is the difference between drifting and driving. And now, you're in the driver's seat.

You've learned how to break big goals into small steps, how to build momentum, how to track progress without discouragement, and how to reroute without quitting. You've learned how to align money with values, how to use technology wisely, how to leverage community, and how to build timelines that turn dreams into dates.

This is what intention looks like in real life:
- You plan before the month starts.
- You review instead of avoid.

• You adjust instead of quit.
• You build instead of react.

Scripture captures this posture perfectly: *"The plans of the diligent lead surely to abundance."* (Proverbs 21:5). Diligence is not hustle—it's **intentional consistency**. And you now have the tools, habits, and mindset to move with purpose, even when life gets loud.

You don't need motivation anymore. You have momentum.

Money Works for You—Not Against You

This is the ultimate shift.

Money is no longer something that happens *to* you.
It is something that works *for* you.

Your cash flow now has assignments. Your debt has deadlines. Your credit has strategy. Your savings has structure. Your future has funding. Money is no longer an emotional enemy—it is a **cooperative tool**.

Instead of draining you, money now supports you.
Instead of stressing you, money now stabilizes you.
Instead of controlling you, money now obeys you.

This doesn't mean you'll never face challenges again. It means challenges no longer knock you off course. You have buffers. You have systems. You have discipline, patience, confidence, and delayed gratification. You have internal strength and external support. You are no longer fragile—you are **financially resilient**.

Scripture declares, *"The borrower is servant to the lender."* (Proverbs 22:7). You read that verse earlier as caution. Now you read it as confirmation—because you are actively breaking servitude and stepping into sovereignty. You are moving from dependence to dominion, from survival to stewardship.

And here's the dopamine truth: once money starts working for you, **winning becomes addictive**. Progress becomes exciting. Discipline becomes empowering. Peace becomes familiar. And you realize—you were never meant to struggle forever.

What's Next: Keep Building, Keep Growing

Financial sovereignty is not a finish line—it's a foundation.

If this book has shifted how you think, imagine what continued education, structure, and community can do. That's why this journey doesn't stop here.

You can continue growing by reading more books by **Rev. Darryl Bass**, each designed to take you deeper—into mindset, identity, wealth-building, emotional healing around money, and generational legacy.

And if you're ready for **guided execution**, accountability, and accelerated results, the **Debt Eliminator Course offered through Savings Solutions** exists for one reason: to help you implement everything you've learned—step by step—until debt is eliminated, credit is strengthened, savings are built, and retirement is no longer a question mark.

You don't need another motivational message.
You need a system you can live inside of.

And now—you're ready for that.

Final Charge

You are no longer surviving.
You are no longer guessing.
You are no longer drifting.

You are **financially sovereign**.

Move forward with confidence.
Move forward with discipline.
Move forward with faith and wisdom.

Your money has a new assignment now.

It works for you.

Other Books by Rev. Darryl Bass

<table>
<tr>
<td>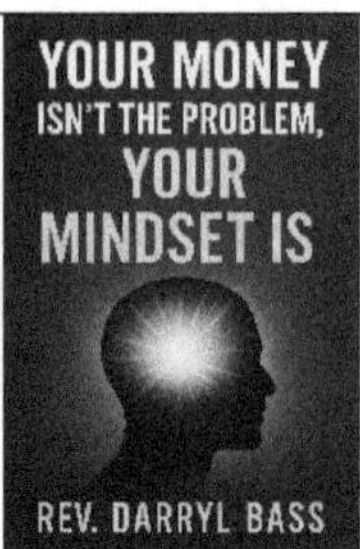
</td>
<td>Your Money Isn’t the Problem, Your Mindset Is

A transformational work that challenges limiting financial beliefs and redefines wealth from the inside out, empowering readers to align their identity with abundance and responsibility.</td>
</tr>
<tr><td></td><td></td></tr>
<tr>
<td>
</td>
<td>This Is Why You’re Broke

A bold and unapologetic examination of the habits, beliefs, and financial behaviors that keep people trapped in cycles of struggle. This book confronts uncomfortable truths and replaces excuses with execution, helping readers shift from reactive spending to strategic wealth building.</td>
</tr>
<tr><td></td><td></td></tr>
<tr>
<td>
</td>
<td>Healing Your Financial Trauma

This book addresses the psychological and emotional roots of money struggles, helping readers break cycles, confront financial pain, and rebuild confidence and stability.</td>
</tr>
<tr><td></td><td></td></tr>
<tr>
<td>
</td>
<td>The Financial Identity Shift

A mindset-and-behavior reset that helps readers align who they are with how they handle money, transforming financial habits through identity-based discipline.</td>
</tr>
</table>

<table>
<tr><td></td><td></td></tr>
<tr><td>
</td><td>The Life Progression System

A comprehensive blueprint for intentional living, The Life Progression System guides readers through structured personal growth, goal alignment, mindset transformation, and legacy building. It equips individuals with practical tools to move from drifting through life to deliberately designing it.</td></tr>
<tr><td></td><td></td></tr>
<tr><td>
</td><td>The Life Progression System Workbook

A comprehensive blueprint for intentional living, The Life Progression System guides readers through structured personal growth, goal alignment, mindset transformation, and legacy building. It equips individuals with practical tools to move from drifting through life to deliberately designing it.</td></tr>
<tr><td></td><td></td></tr>
<tr><td>
</td><td>Borrowed Futures

A wake-up call about the hidden costs of debt and financial shortcuts, showing readers how to escape debt cycles and build futures without financial bondage.</td></tr>
<tr><td></td><td></td></tr>
<tr><td>
</td><td>Life Insurance: The Gift of Life After Life

More than a policy explanation, this book reframes life insurance as a strategic wealth-building and legacy-protection tool. It educates families on how to use life insurance for income replacement, debt protection, estate planning, generational wealth transfer, and financial leverage.</td></tr>
<tr><td></td><td></td></tr>
</table>

<table>
<tr>
<td>
</td>
<td>The Intellectual Property Wealth Blueprint

A strategic guide to turning knowledge into income, this book teaches creators how to package ideas into books, courses, systems, and assets that generate scalable and recurring revenue streams.</td>
</tr>
<tr>
<td></td>
<td></td>
</tr>
<tr>
<td>
</td>
<td>The Intellectual Property Wealth Blueprint 2.0
Focused on licensing, certification, and legacy systems, this volume expands intellectual property into scalable enterprises that create long-term wealth and generational ownership structures.</td>
</tr>
</table>

The Debt Eliminator
Coming 2026

What if 2026 was the year everything changed?

What if this was the year you stopped surviving… and started building?
The year you stopped juggling bills… and started creating wealth?
The year debt stopped controlling your decisions?

The **Debt Eliminator** is not another budgeting class.
It is a structured financial transformation system designed to help individuals and families break free from consumer debt, rebuild financial confidence, and establish a foundation for long-term wealth.

This course was built for hardworking people who are tired of living paycheck to paycheck. It was created for families who want stability, not stress. It was designed for individuals who know they are capable of more—but need a system that works.

What the Debt Eliminator Will Teach You:

• How to eliminate consumer debt strategically and aggressively
• How to increase income without adding overwhelm
• How to rebuild and optimize your credit profile
• How to build savings while eliminating debt
• How to structure emergency funds and protection plans
• How to shift your financial identity from borrower to builder
• How to create systems that prevent debt from returning

This is not theory.
This is execution.

Through step-by-step modules, implementation tools, accountability structure, and real-life application, you will learn how to take control of your money instead of letting it control you.

Imagine waking up without financial anxiety.
Imagine having a plan.
Imagine watching your balances decrease and your confidence increase.
Imagine positioning your household for ownership, investing, and generational legacy.

That transformation begins in 2026.

The Debt Eliminator is more than a course.
It is a movement toward financial clarity, discipline, and freedom.

Get ready to break cycles.
Get ready to build stability.
Get ready to eliminate debt—permanently.

The Debt Eliminator — Launching 2026.

Join our waiting list Today!
https://savingssolution.org/join

The Financial Freedom Revolution Tour

Launching 2026

This is not a seminar.
This is not a motivational rally.
This is a financial awakening.

The **Financial Freedom Revolution Tour** is a live, high-impact experience designed to ignite transformation in individuals, families, entrepreneurs, and communities ready to break financial cycles and build generational stability.

For too long, people have been working harder but falling further behind. Income rises. Expenses rise. Stress rises. Yet true financial progress feels out of reach.

The Revolution changes that.

This national tour brings together powerful teaching, real strategy, live coaching, and structured execution plans that move attendees from confusion to clarity—and from debt to disciplined wealth-building.

What You'll Experience:

• A clear roadmap to financial stability and long-term wealth
• Step-by-step strategies for eliminating consumer debt
• Income growth frameworks and entrepreneurship positioning
• Credit optimization and financial leverage strategies
• Protection planning and legacy-building principles
• Live financial assessments and actionable implementation steps

• A mindset shift from survival thinking to ownership thinking

This is not inspiration without structure.
This is strategy with accountability.

The Financial Freedom Revolution Tour is built for families who want peace instead of pressure. For entrepreneurs who want profit with structure. For leaders who understand that financial stability is the foundation for community impact.

Imagine thousands gathered in one space—learning, planning, committing to real change.
Imagine leaving with a clear blueprint instead of just excitement.
Imagine knowing exactly what steps to take the next day.

This is more than an event.
It is a declaration that debt cycles end here.
It is a call to financial responsibility, ownership, and generational leadership.

Cities across the country will host this movement in 2026.

Seats will fill.
Lives will shift.
Legacies will be built.

The Financial Freedom Revolution Tour — Coming 2026.

This is the year you stop reacting to money
…and start commanding it.

The revolution begins with one decision.
https://savingssolution.org/tour

Follow on Social Media

Facebook:

https://www.facebook.com/LPSCoach

Twitter:

https://twitter.com/LPS_Coach

Instagram:

https://www.instagram.com/lps_coach/

YouTube:

https://www.youtube.com/@life_progression_system

TikTok:

https://www.tiktok.com/@debt_annihilator

LinkedIn:

https://www.linkedin.com/in/lpscoach/

www.ingramcontent.com/pod-product-compliance
Lightning Source LLC
LaVergne TN
LVHW020702110826
845149LV00012B/2079

* 9 7 8 1 9 7 2 1 1 5 1 8 3 *